# Intruding on Academe

# Intruding

*on*

# Academe

*The Assertion of Political Control in Illinois*

Jack R. Van Der Slik

Southern Illinois University Press
*Carbondale and Edwardsville*

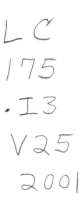
Library of Congress Cataloging-in-Publication Data

    Van Der Slik, Jack R., 1936–
    Intruding on academe : the assertion of political control in
Illinois / Jack R. Van Der Slik.
        p. cm.
    Includes bibliographical references (p. ) and index.
      1. Higher education and state—Illinois.  2. Education, Higher—
Illinois—Administration.  3. Education, Higher—Law and legislation—
Illinois.  I. Title.
    LC175.I3 V25 2001
    379.773—dc21                              00-026556
    ISBN 0-8093-2349-4 (alk. paper)

*For David T. Kenney and David H. Everson*

# Contents

# Preface

The Republican electoral resurgence of November 1994 made the restructuring of higher education governance in Illinois a likelihood. I recognized that prospect at a propitious moment. Recently, I had brought to completion a study of the Illinois congressional delegation (1995), and I was in search of a scholarly project that would permit me to examine legislative and executive relations in Illinois. Because I knew many of the players in the higher education policy sphere, it was my judgment that I could learn a great deal by means of in-depth interviews while the issue was being dealt with in the political arena. So during 1995 while the restructuring process went forward in the legislature, I undertook a series of conversations with many of the principal participants.

Conducting the interviews was the most pleasurable part of my study. Because all the interviewees are named in the book, I'll not repeat them here. But I must say that I found the players accessible, well informed, open, articulate, candid, helpful, and fair minded. I was especially impressed by the realistic and pacific analyses I received from the chancellors whose systems were being dissolved into oblivion during the very time of our interviews. In short, the respondents were a classy group of people from whom I enriched my understanding about Illinois politics. I thank them for the generous interviews as well as for reviewing the written typescripts and returning them corrected and improved in a timely fashion. In every case, these people confirmed how much more efficiently one can work with busy people than with persons of greater leisure and lesser responsibilities.

The difficult part of the book was in making the nuggets of information fit together in a meaningful interpretation. As my scholarly citations indicate, I particularly benefited from works by John Kingdon, Charles O. Jones, Frank Baumgartner, and Bryan D. Jones. Both Chuck Jones and Frank Baumgartner gave me encouraging feedback on a précis of this monograph. I also received good advice from anonymous reviewers whose professionalism I much appreciated. Closer to home, I had the support of colleagues at the University of Illinois at Springfield who diligently critiqued early drafts. And I appreciate the generous help I received from Carol Everly Floyd, Lee Frost-Kumpf, David Joens, Kent D. Redfield, Doh C. Shin, and Ed Wojcicki.

Despite the brevity of this book, the research and interviews necessitated a great amount of word processing, correspondence, and organizational support. I was blessed with excellent professional assistance from Cheryl Eckland, Lorrie Farrington, and Elizabeth Kniery, but my thanks go especially to Ann Aldrich and Kathy Bottoms, who did the bulk of the work and without whom this project would not have been completed. Nancy Ford, executive director of the Institute for Public Affairs and Administration, provided the necessary support through the Illinois Legislative Studies Center. Not least, I counted on my wife, Bonnie, to handle correspondence and electronic transmission of drafts after we relocated from Springfield, Illinois, to Port St. Lucie, Florida.

This book is dedicated to two colleagues named David, who have enlarged the intellectual horizons of my life. David T. Kenney opened my eyes to the richness of Illinois politics during my years with him as director of the Public Affairs Research Bureau at Southern Illinois University Carbondale. Over a fruitful career in Illinois, Kenney has been for me a model at both scholarly inquiry and political participation, pursuing each with self-sacrificing integrity. David H. Everson was for nearly all my professional life both peer and pal. We began our careers together at SIUC on July 1, 1967. We toiled together there and at Sangamon State University (now the University of Illinois at Springfield) in a great many projects, problems, and pleasures until his untimely death in 1999. I miss both his wit and wisdom about all manner of Illinois matters.

To these book-loving exemplars in my life, I dedicate this book.

# Intruding on Academe

# 1 | An Overview of the Restructuring of Higher Education in Illinois

§ hortly before the completion of Jim Edgar's second term as governor of Illinois, a book entitled *Meeting the Challenge: The Edgar Administration 1991–1999* was published under his direction to mark the administration's accomplishments. One achievement that is described in some detail is "the restructuring of the administration of Illinois' public universities. What resulted was the most far-reaching change in university governance in Illinois since the 1960's" (Schafer 1998, 43). Unquestionably, this was a policy change of major significance, and it was one in which the governor played a prominent leadership role. But it was a change not easily executed. It had to transcend the political checks and balances of a highly partisan major state.

One means of learning and explaining the political processes is to examine with care the complex actions implicit in policy-making. This particular one brings together images of bureaucratic behavior, interest group action, legislative give and take, Illinois regionalism, partisanship, and, importantly, executive leadership. The case and its analysis reveal, I believe, a good deal about how Illinois' politics works. But this case is not a deviant case. To the contrary, I intend to demonstrate that it is understandable because its major lines have a good fit with previously developed theoretical explanations of public policy-making.

Restructuring higher education in Illinois exemplifies changes noted nationally. William Zumeta (1998) recently observed that "reticence by state leaders to become involved in higher education policy has been replaced by much more salience and concern as the economic and social importance of higher education has grown, as state government's capacity for data collection and analysis has increased, and as elected and appointed officials with college education and more have shown less deference to, or trust in, the learned souls of the academy" (11). Zumeta argues that the pace of intrusion by policymakers has been "picking up noticeably," using themes of efficiency and accountability. "Policymakers are no longer hesitant to advance proposals, however flawed and limited, to seek to ensure such results" (12). For career academics, both administrators and faculty, the implications of this changed policy environment are not yet clear in Illinois or elsewhere. For academics throughout the American states, the case may raise both fascination and dread concerning what mischief the politicians could do in "my state" if they took it into their minds to intrude on the universities in like fashion. For political activists the question may be raised, How much responsibility can you exercise over the knowledge industry and still obtain political benefit? The case study that follows may provide careerists in both academia and politics a larger information base for their calculations.

The political players are a familiar lot: the governor of Illinois and others in his administration and members of the legislature including House and Senate Democrats and Republicans. The education policy experts are higher education bureaucrats and campus presidents. There are "in between" players who work for the education bureaucrats by lobbying the political decisionmakers.

The policy problem under consideration here is small enough to comprehend the whole thing. Yet there are enough nuances and players to make the telling interesting. The issue moves. Players make plays. Some of those plays work, and some do not. There is give and take, compromise and adjustment, the very kind of compromise that is central to the way politics "really" works. Some of the plays are "inside," not subject to public view. But, as is so central to American representative democracy, real decisions have to be made in the public arena with the players "on the record" and accountable to the citizens and voters for what they do.

My approach in this study has two parts. The first part is to simply report the story of how higher education governance has been conducted in recent decades and how that changed in 1995. This moving picture is the setup piece for the rest of the book. It is told from the public record of published articles and news reports and has a chronological story line.

The second part is more elaborate and has two elements to illuminate the first part. The first element is theory. Are there patterns familiar to analysts of policy-making in American politics that are present in this case study? Does looking for pattern fitting behavior help me understand and explain what happened in this case? After that, perhaps, I can turn the explanatory argument around. What in this case study may help to clarify, elaborate, or streamline political scientists' understanding of how "government and politics really work"? Because I am examining a single case study, it would be too strong to say I am going to "test" theory by systematic analysis of falsifiable hypotheses. But there is some informative literature about policy-making whose insights I will use to analyze this case. So I will work back and forth between theory and my information from the case to understand not only the case but also the politics of policy-making.

The second element in this study to illuminate the case is a large amount of data. The data for my study are mostly from in-depth interviews with persons intimately involved in this policy-making case. As a longtime close observer of Illinois politics, I had access not only to formal proceedings at the capitol but also to a fair acquaintance with many of the players conspicuous in the news accounts of the story. As a faculty member at Sangamon State University and, previously, Southern Illinois University at Carbondale, I have observed the "system of systems," which will be described, over a substantial period. As an administrator and faculty representative, I have been close to the workings of the Board of Regents system and the board of higher education. On the basis of knowing which players were substantively engaged in the issue, I was able to conduct a series of interviews with persons engaged in the policy process. Between February and December 1995, I interviewed twenty-five persons, all of whom were substantially engaged with this issue. Only two people I wanted access to were unavailable: the governor, for understandable reasons, and the board chair for one of the university systems. However, the governor's office was very helpful, allowing on-the-record interviews with the governor's press chief and the governor's higher education staffer. Moreover, Lieutenant Governor Bob Kustra, the administration's primary spokesperson on this issue, provided a wide-ranging interview. Instead of the system's board chair, who was unavailable, I interviewed the university system legislative liaison.

The quality of the interview data is excellent. All the interviewers were candid and forthcoming. They came from the entire spectrum of participants (names and titles are listed at the end of chapter 3): the governor's administration, both parties and chambers of the legislature, and diverse education participants. There was not a singular interview protocol, but all were interviewed "on the record" and at length about their parts in the policy process and their observations and interpretations of the changes in progress. All interviews were recorded and transcribed. Interviewees were later asked to review the transcription and correct it. Only minor, mostly stylistic, revisions resulted, and in one interview, the source requested that two brief passages be treated as background information and "not for attribution." I will draw upon portions from these interviews as data to explain the case and to look for fit with patterns drawn from earlier research.

The roots of policy are hard to trace with precision. John W. Kingdon (1984) observed that "when we try to track down the origins of an idea or proposal, we become involved in an infinite regress. An idea doesn't start with the proximate source. It has a history. When one starts to trace the history of a proposal or concern back through time, there is no logical place to stop the process" (77). Certainly, this observation applies to my attempt to describe and analyze the restructuring of higher education in Illinois in 1995. There are key points in the event chronology. I will use the public record to try to capture them.

## Developing Illinois' System of Systems

Higher education is big business in Illinois. In 1995, there were 12 public universities, 49 public community colleges, and 103 nonpublic institutions (Ryan 1997, 100). The changing dynamics of higher education are suggested by noting that in 1951, Illinois had a head count enrollment of fewer than 127,000 students. Of those students, 25.4 percent (over 32,000) attended public universities, 10.5 percent (over 13,000) attended community colleges, and 64.0 percent (over 81,000) attended private institutions. By peak enrollment in 1991, the total served was

756,000, with 26.7 percent (over 202,000) in public universities, 48.7 percent (over 368,000) in community colleges, and 24.6 percent (over 185,000) in private institutions. (Illinois Board of Higher Education 1997, 91).

Until after World War II, the state had only one state university, with a single main campus: the University of Illinois Urbana Champaign. But as recent commentators (Nowlan and Gove 1991) observed: "The obscure teachers college at Carbondale in deep southern Illinois was the first to break the normal school mold. Combining an ambitious new president, postwar demand, regionalism, and political leverage in the legislature, the college transformed itself into Southern Illinois University, with more than 36,000 students in 1990 on two campuses in Carbondale and Edwardsville and a medical school in Springfield" (124). SIU administrators would additionally point with pride to a wide variety of off-campus programs, a school of dental medicine in Alton, Illinois, and a budding campus in Nakejo, Japan.

In 1959, a political deal was struck in which the patron legislators for the U of I and SIU, Senator Everett Peters and House Speaker Paul Powell, laid the groundwork for a Chicago campus for the U of I and the Edwardsville campus for SIU. The rivalry between the U of I and SIU heightened expectations as other normal schools became universities. According to Gove and Floyd (1973): "In 1961 the legislature, unable to cope with policy making in this competitive situation, created the Illinois Board of Higher Education. The IBHE was specifically charged with program approval, budget review and master-planning" (287). They go on to argue that political leaders gave two reasons for establishing the IBHE. First, the legislature did not want to pick winners and losers in the rivalries among the universities. Second, specialized expertise was needed to conduct an orderly expansion of programs while minimizing expensive program duplication.

When the IBHE was established in 1961, it oversaw three governing boards: the board of U of I, one for SIU, and the Teachers College Board. The latter governed what are now Northern Illinois University, Illinois State University, Eastern Illinois University, and Western Illinois University. In 1965, as part of Master Plan I, the IBHE recommended the establishment of a board to plan and coordinate a system of community colleges that would, like the university boards, be subject to its oversight. Two Chicago colleges, now known as Chicago State University and Northeastern Illinois University, were transferred from the city of Chicago to the state of Illinois to be governed by the Teachers College Board, itself now named the Board of Governors of State Colleges and Universities. Following the IBHE's Master Plan II in 1966, NIU and ISU were to develop a broad range of doctoral programs in arts and sciences and so were separated from the more narrowly defined state universities. NIU and ISU were placed under a new governing board, the Board of Regents. During the late 1960s, despite opposition from private colleges and universities (Floyd 1992, 106), plans went forward for two new, upper-division (for junior, senior, and graduate students) universities— one in the Chicago area and one in Springfield. These senior universities were planned to provide degree completion programs for junior college graduates. In 1969, Sangamon State University and Governors State University were authorized by the legislature—SSU subject to the BOR and GSU under the BOG. During this era of diversification in higher education, both the U of I and SIU made unsuccessful political efforts to discourage such expansion as well as to make SSU part of their universities (Floyd 1992). The substance of these changes was to establish a system of systems. IBHE coordinated the activities and programming for four university systems (U of I, SIU, the BOR, and the BOG) and the community college board. It also provided a typological categorization of the higher education systems:

- The fully developed complex, multipurpose university (U of I)
- The rapidly developing complex, multipurpose university (SIU)
- The liberal arts universities (NIU and ISU)
- The state universities and colleges of more limited scope than the liberal arts universities
- Community colleges

This categorization further constituted a division of power with checks and balances that the IBHE argued would serve higher education well in Illinois (Illinois Board of Higher Education 1967, 38–39).

During the 1970s, the politics of higher education shifted in Illinois. The governor's budgetary powers became more central and controlling. Illinois rewrote its constitution in 1970, giving the governor not only conventional veto power but also the item veto, amendatory veto, and item reduction veto. The governor, Richard Ogilvie, strengthened his own staff by creating a Bureau of the Budget. In 1971, the IBHE aggressively recommended a large, nearly 33 percent, increase in general revenue funds for higher education over the preceding year in its FY 72 budget. The IBHE executive director, despite contrary advice from the governor's budget bureau, stuck to his request. The governor responded with a budget proposal requesting less than a 1 percent increase. Both sides appealed to the legislature, which was accustomed to ratifying consensus worked out in advance. The legislature responded with a compromise, passing a 10 percent increase. However, the governor insistently reduced the appropriations down to his original recommendations, and efforts in the legislature to restore its level of funding failed (Nowlan and Gove 1991, 128–30). To add insult to injury, the governor reduced the IBHE's own administrative office appropriations bill 43 percent below that for the previous year (Floyd 1992, 112, 117; see also Pensoneau 1997, 171–78, 183–84, for more on the personalities of the participants).

Although there have been occasional deviations, between 1971 and the 1990s, the higher education appropriations process followed a normal pattern. The individual universities would propose their budgets to their system, such as the BOR.

The system office would trim and repackage the requests, submitting them each fall to the IBHE. The IBHE executive director would reduce the requests to a number considered defensible within current political vagaries. The board would approve and forward that recommendation to the governor. Then the governor and the Bureau of the Budget would make a recommendation, usually a few percentage points higher than the higher education budget for the preceding year. These amounts would be rendered into appropriations bills for legislative enactment. From time to time, legislative actions would tack on some extra dollars, but not with regularity. Typical budgetary outcomes for the universities resulted not from campus initiatives but according to macroeconomic considerations in the state and how much the governor would need in any given budget year for other priorities. Higher education budgets were driven incrementally rather than programmatically (for more details about the 1970s, see Nowlan 1976, 68–77, 92–100; see also Nowlan and Gove 1991, 123–36).

## Checks and Balances as a Working Model

After its budgetary whipping in FY 72, the IBHE turned its regulatory attention to the universities. Public universities were required to identify "low-priority" programs that might be eliminated to allow reallocation of 15 percent of operating funds to high-priority programs. The reluctance of the universities to comply led the IBHE staff to draw upon campus originated program reviews in order to identify its own list of low-priority programs. Bickering back and forth between IBHE, system staffs, and campus university administrators about programs resulted in a practice of program review that left the power to prioritize in the hands of governing systems—a "shared responsibilities approach," as Rod Groves, chancellor of the BOR, called it (Floyd 1992, 112). Universities reviewed programs on five- to eight-year cycles, and some weak programs were eliminated. The IBHE nagged the universities with comparative cost studies per student credit hour by disciplines. IBHE recommendations concerning program elimination stirred action on the campuses—sometimes to strengthen such programs and often to streamline or eliminate them. As the dialogue moved back and forth and as IBHE gathered detailed institutional data from recurring program reviews, new program requests, and proposals for expansion, IBHE's ability to finger weak or expensive programs on campuses was undeniable. But the authority to recommend program termination was rarely exercised by IBHE, so the hard choices still had to be made at the governing board and campus levels. According to one insider: "Two factors moderated the level of governmental and legislative pressures on IBHE during the 1980s. First, though economic conditions were not rosy, appropriations levels permitted modest growth in some years and required no major retrenchment. Second, no political actors proposed to reorganize higher education by increasing the powers of the coordinating board or by replacing the coordinating board and governing boards with a single superboard" (Floyd 1992, 114).

Floyd's second point, about political actors, is only true if limited to major political actors. Over the years, there were a number of legislators who proposed bills to tinker with the system of systems, to alter the scope and independence of the universities, and to enlarge or to trim the powers of the governing boards or the IBHE. In 1983, House Bill 700 was intended as major surgery; it came rather close to legislative enactment. In 1989, legislative supporters of NIU and ISU tried to achieve separate governance for their schools. A minor change in governance was granted those two schools in 1990, providing each "their" alumnus on the BOR. In 1991, major changes were proposed in the legislature but, without leader support, went nowhere. In 1992, the focus was enlarged to both the BOR and the BOG, but legislative leaders never let the bills out of the leader-dominated rules committee.

The academic community had its own debate about the system of systems in *Illinois Issues*. The opening salvo came from Albert Somit (1987), who had recently stepped down from the presidency of SIUC. As the IBHE was marking its twenty-fifth anniversary, Somit offered six rather sweeping criticisms, of which four focused on the IBHE and two on the system of systems, as follows:

- The IBHE is more concerned with protecting private higher education than in furthering public higher education.
- The IBHE has become a compliant tool of the governor that limits spending for higher education.
- The IBHE is increasingly ineffectual in policy leadership for public higher education.
- IBHE budget recommendations favor the University of Illinois.
- The system of systems bureaucracy is needlessly expensive.
- The system of systems constitutes an irrational organization of 12 public universities.

Somit offered some supporting data and explanations for his points, arguing that economies could be achieved by a restructuring. His solution would be a two-system model, likened to the "California model." One would include "all institutions with a primary graduate education mission" and the second, "all other senior institutions." The first category would be UIUC, UIC, SIUC, and NIU. This system would be known as the U of I. The remaining eight schools would be administered by the IBHE, "with the board and staff suitably renamed and reconstituted."

The debate was joined a month later, in the next issue of *Illinois Issues,* by James M. Furman (1987), who seven years earlier had left the executive directorship of the IBHE. Furman refuted Somit point by point, describing IBHE as effective and professional and suggesting that any proposed savings on bureaucratic changes might be "dwarfed by the inefficiencies that . . . greater centralization and . . . major organizational changes" might bring. Furman dismissed the California model both for not always working well in California as well as for being the solution to the wrong problem. Furman noted the experience of Wisconsin, "which moved from the 'California system' to the 'New York system' in the early 1970s." He concluded that "changing the structure of higher education tends to become an overwhelming distraction for both the institutions involved and the political leadership of the state," diverting energy and attention away from substantive problems and toward divisive structural issues.

In January 1988, *Illinois Issues* published comments on the Somit and Furman articles by the IBHE executive director, four system heads, the executive director of the community college board, and four campus CEOs ("Higher Education: Other Views" 1988). (Titles like president and chancellor are not used because they meant different things in different systems—perhaps the least significant of the irrationalities Somit noted.) Most shot Somit's proposal down or damned it with faint praise. The campus CEOs Somit proposed to put with the U of I were not agreeable. UIC preferred the Furman view. The NIU position was to seek its fortune pursuing a unique mission. There was no new voice for SIUC, but its system head saw the current structure as being "as sensible as that of any of the states." ISU's CEO resented being omitted from the research universities but argued that funding for all the universities was more important than structural alignments. Stanley Ikenberry, system head for the U of I, and clearly the then heavyweight champion of Illinois higher education, said substantive issues and financial deprivation were the real problems and that the current governance system "served the people of Illinois well."

A month later, Somit acknowledged little support from current higher education leaders, insisting that "yes, the system 'works'—but not very well" ("Higher Education's System of Systems" 1988). James C. Worthy, one of the architects of the system of systems weighed in. He acknowledged the pragmatic organizational decisions of the past and allowed that "a structure that was appropriate nearly a generation ago may now need modification and perhaps extensive revision. . . ." But he cautioned that any restructure would be "dealing with an extremely complex subject involving major vested interests, keen institutional rivalries, and controversial issues of high emotional content." Lastly, a couple of ISU administrators subjected some of Somit's data on the various universities to cluster analysis, arguing empirically that Somit's proposed two classes of universities was "itself not immune to the charge of structural irrationality." The clear weight of opinion by the players in the academic world during 1988 was that the system was not broken and that trying to structurally remake it was a waste of time and effort.

In March 1989, Governor James R. Thompson noted that it was time for challenging and renewing Illinois higher education. He asked the IBHE to examine issues of accountability and productivity (Illinois Board of Higher Education 1990). The IBHE responded by creating a "Committee on Scope, Structure, and Productivity of Illinois Higher Education." Of the twenty-three members, eight were from the board itself. There were four legislators (aptly, one from each party in each chamber), all of whom were held in high regard in their respective caucuses for education expertise. Others included six from a variety of academic positions in both private and public higher education, one lobbyist (Illinois Coalition), one state government insider (commissioner of banks and former state senator), and two Illinois corporate executives. The chair was James M. Furman, from the MacArthur Foundation and the former IBHE executive director, who had refuted Somit's critique of the system of systems. The committee reviewed written presentations from a variety of education advocates, published works, and reports from IBHE staff. The resulting report dealt with the three topics of scope, structure, and productivity. However, the portion on structure, shortest of the three, was mostly a description of Illinois' complex governance system and a rationale for retaining it. Options for change mentioned were either more boards or fewer boards, leaving the then current arrangements looking like the golden mean. While the committee urged a variety of actions on the IBHE to enlarge access to higher education and aggressive steps to improve quality, cost effectiveness, and accountability, structure was not seen to be a problem. The committee recommended the following resolution: "The Board of Higher Education finds no compelling reason to change the existing organizational structure of Illinois higher education and concludes that the structure should be retained. Creating additional governing boards for individual public universities would unnecessarily complicate the structure of Illinois higher education. Reducing the number of public university governing boards may offer some advantages but the effort to restructure governing boards would significantly detract from efforts to carry out the program goals of Illinois higher education." On May 1, 1990, the report was adopted by the IBHE, setting a framework for a major exercise in the public universities, known as PQP (Priorities, Quality, and Productivity). Presumably, the higher education community was prepared for a variety of issues in the 1990s, but the specifics of governance restructuring were off the table, with consensual support from a diverse set of education players in the private sector, the legislature, and the public universities.

Despite the election of a new governor in 1990 and the establishment of a new administration in 1991, initially there were not significant actions on higher education restructuring. Governor Edgar focused on the budget and making permanent a previously passed temporary income tax rate increase. Perhaps Edgar's most significant action regarding higher education in the beginning of his term was appointment of Art Quern to be the chair of IBHE. Quern, who earlier had been chief of staff to Governor James Thompson, was to become a major force in changing higher education policy. But policy initiation was not immediate. The governance bills introduced to the legislature that year indicated that not everyone agreed with the prevailing policy consensus, but none of the legislators who introduced them had backing from major players. So no bills were even called for a vote on passage in chambers of origin.

## Changes for Higher Education on the Agenda

The legislative milieu changed on January 27, 1992, when Governor Edgar included in his state of the state address the idea that the governing boards for two systems, the BOR and the BOG, be abolished and that Sangamon State might be made part of the U of I. Two and a half months later, the governor moved the issue further in his budget message. He said his proposed budget would protect funding for higher education from cuts imposed on the rest of state government, but he would appoint a task force to reduce administrative costs and put more money into classroom expenditures. Edgar's directions were clear: "I want the task force to focus particularly on whether the current system, which includes several governing boards, should be streamlined." He promised a preliminary report by June 1, before the end of the legislative session. The ten-member task force was cochaired by Lieutenant Governor Bob Kustra and Art Quern, Edgar's recently appointed chair of the IBHE. Appointees included attorneys at two major Chicago law firms, one former member of the U of I Board of Trustees, and five corporate executives from around the state. The task force focused mostly upon earlier written reports and "written testimony from governing board members, college and university presidents and system heads, public university faculty senate representatives, faculty union representatives, private higher education representatives and student organizations" (Governor's Task Force on Higher Education 1992). There was only one public hearing, which "was scheduled only after the [Bloomington] *Pantagraph* and United Press International ran stories questioning the scope of the task force's review and its secret deliberations" (Thompson 1992). According to Thompson, Kustra noted that the hearing "added nothing new to the record."

The Kustra-Quern task force recommended downsizing current system offices and budgets along with placing more authority with the universities and the IBHE, away from the system offices. The task force then proposed two structural options. Option 1 would organize the system by types of institutions and mission.

> This option would decrease the number of governing boards by one, but more importantly would provide focus and attention to doctoral-granting institutions within one governing body and a regional undergraduate focus within another governing board. This organization would leave the two current campuses with the University of Illinois and add Springfield (Sangamon State University), combine the entire Southern Illinois University system with Northern Illinois University and Illinois State University and place Chicago State University, Eastern Illinois University, Governors State University, Northeastern Illinois University, and Western Illinois University within one system.
>
> A second option is to move towards decentralization and organize a system by region with strong oversight functions by the Board of Higher Education. Although new governing boards would be established, sys-

tem offices would be eliminated and very skeletal staffs would provide support to the boards through the offices of the campus presidents.

This organization would establish a new board (located in Chicago) to govern Chicago State University, Governors State University and Northeastern Illinois University with a focus on urban educational opportunities. Separate governing boards would be established for Northern Illinois University, Illinois State University, Eastern Illinois University and Western Illinois University. Except for the addition of Sangamon State University to the University of Illinois, the current structure of the systems of the University of Illinois and Southern Illinois University would remain unchanged. (Governor's Task Force on Higher Education 1993)

Additionally, the report called for the governor to appoint members of the U of I board rather than selection by statewide partisan elections. It urged a change in IBHE membership so that none of those members would simultaneously serve on the governing boards of particular universities.

Besides the news coverage of the task force report and various responses to it, there were two major journalistic reports. *Crain's Chicago Business* touted arguments for downsizing and restructuring higher education as has happened in industry and, to some extent, the public schools (Coleman 1992). According to *Crain's,* if they scrutinized universities, business executives would find the following:

1. Campus spending priorities are skewed, rewarding educrats at the expense of students.
2. Bureaucracy costs are mounting.
3. Program duplication abounds, total faculty teaching loads are dropping, and productivity levels need scrutiny.
4. Public and private competition is heating up, spurring more spending and duplication.

While a variety of commentators were cited, prominence was given to the views of Kustra and Quern. The article concludes with Quern indicating why academicians should promptly get about the business of reshaping their institutions: "If they're not up the task, we'll have to come in with a business-discipline approach. We may have to be more aggressive. And once you have businessmen in there (analyzing costs and management structures), they may wish they could have handled it themselves" (32).

Under the banner "Degrees of Neglect" (Grossman, Jouzaitis, and Leroux 1992), the *Chicago Tribune* ran a long and substantive front-page series beginning with the headline "Our Failing Colleges." Although citing authorities from around the country, much of the attention was on Illinois public universities and their deficiencies. The title of the first report was "Students Get Shortchanged as Schools Vie for Dollars." The teasers for the subsequent stories were "Why Bigger Isn't

Necessarily Better in Higher Education," "Research Has Replaced Instruction as the Dominant Missions of Academics," "The Lure of Easy Federal Money Shaped Higher Education in the 1980s," and "Some Administrators Are Beginning to Appreciate the Lost Art of Teaching." The *Chicago Tribune* pieces leveled no particular criticism at governance but strongly suggested that accountability for strong undergraduate education is lacking, particularly in Illinois state universities.

Administrators on the various state university campuses recall this time period in 1992 as one of considerable stress. The PQP process of review was in its first year of implementation. All the campuses had received a series of recommended actions from the IBHE staff. Those included recommendations for program reductions and, in some cases, for the elimination of programs.

The legislature did no more on higher education structure, preoccupied as it was by the budget battle between Governor Edgar and House Speaker Michael Madigan. A stringent budget was adopted, eased by no new taxes or fees, following a fiscal year (FY 92) in which the shortfall from spending over revenues was estimated at $900 million (Wheeler 1992). Political anticipation was all about the legislative results in November, when all House and Senate seats would be up in the first election after redistricting.

There was little public discussion on or news about restructuring higher education during the summer and fall of 1992, but the usually invisible statewide election of trustees to the U of I board was somewhat unusual. At least two of the Republican candidates spent substantial amounts of money, one conceding her estimated spending at $30,000. Nevertheless, all three Democrats prevailed. In the statewide electorate, straight party ballots by Democratic voters totaled 805,649. The comparable total for Republicans was 629,685, a party difference of 175,964. The difference between the average vote for the three Democrats and the three Republicans was nearly 423,000 votes, a partisan difference exceeding the straight ticket advantage gained by the Democrats that year. Commentators on the election, Samuel Gove and Thomas Lamont, the board chair, reportedly agreed that "it was clear that party affiliation made the difference in the race" (Wurth 1992). The nine-member board, elected to staggered six-year terms, now favored Democrats by a 6 to 3 margin.

The final report of the Governor's Task Force on Higher Education (1993) was released on January 27, 1993, the day Governor Edgar delivered his state of the state speech. Seven changes were recommended. The primary one was to dissolve the BOR and the BOG and their staffs, creating separate boards for each of seven schools and assigning Sangamon State to become a campus of the U of I. Boards would be appointed by the governor with consent of the Senate. The U of I's board would be changed from elective to appointive. More autonomy would go to the universities, but the coordinative role of the IBHE was to be continued or even strengthened if necessary. Finally, the IBHE board membership would be changed to have more public members, none of whom would concurrently serve on specific school governing boards. Predictably, the chancellors of BOG and BOR were critical of the governor's plan (Pokorski 1993d). U of I President Ikenberry was described in Champaign-Urbana as "generally receptive to the idea of absorbing Sangamon State" (Wurth 1993), while in Carbondale, the system chancellor expressed disappointment that Sangamon State would not go to SIU. According to news reports, the medical school faculty there was pleased (Mattmiller 1993), although medical school administrators in Springfield were disappointed. All participants recognized that details remained to be decided by the legislature.

The partisan composition of the legislature was to shape the handling of the governor's higher education proposal. After more than a decade of Democratic control, the Senate had a Republican majority of 32 to 27. However, the House was still controlled by Democrats, 67 to 51. It was noteworthy that Democratic Speaker Madigan created a joint committee, comprised of members of the House Higher Education Committee and the House Education Appropriations Committee, to consider "both the instructional quality and fiscal accountability" of governor's proposals (Finke and Fitzgerald 1993). The committee would hold hearings statewide.

The key hearing was March 11, and the main witness was Lieutenant Governor Bob Kustra, the governor's designated advocate for the restructuring proposal incorporated into Senate Bill 987. With him were three witnesses, including two members of the governor's task force. After formal presentations, several Democrats vigorously challenged Kustra in particular (Pokorski 1993c). Committee chair Bill Edley, whose constituency included WIU, challenged assertions that the reorganization would save money by reducing bureaucracy. Kustra insisted that some savings would result but that responsiveness by the universities was the important area of improvement. Representative Michael Curran from Springfield charged that boards were being abolished because the BOG, whose institutions included EIU, forced out its president, Stanley Rives. Rives was a friend and political supporter of EIU's notable alumnus and governor, Jim Edgar. Curran's view was that the restructuring was an elaborate payback to punish those who hurt the governor's friend and that Kustra himself had been "told to do this" (House Higher Education Committee Hearing 1993, 31). Kustra responded that his motives grew out of an epiphany he experienced in Macomb, where, as lieutenant governor, he had given a speech and spoken to the mayor:

> It occurred to me something had to be done about the reorganization [of the] system. . . . I went back to my Governor and I said you know, I don't like the system, I don't like the way it works. . . . My governor never told me to do this. . . . I'm absolutely committed to higher education and I resent anybody saying that I'm here carrying the Governor's water on this one . . . this has nothing to do with anything I am doing for the Governor or was instructed to do. I went to him and said, can we create a task force, will you appoint me as the co-chairman. He said, I'll put Art Quern on with you. We did that. I sat down with these people, this wasn't any agenda of Jim Edgar's. (31–32)

While the Republican dominated Senate moved the restructure legislation forward, House Democrats heard from opponents, including BOR executive Rod Groves and board chair Brewster Parker (Pokorski 1993a). Groves argued that the existing system of systems was a balanced and equitable one and that the proposed shift would put over half of the appropriations and a third of the students into the U of I system to the great disadvantage of the other schools and the students attending them.

A subplot in the restructuring drama was about the future for SSU. Smallest of the state universities, it was never thought of as mergeable with the other two schools in the regents system, NIU or ISU. Its capital location could add visibility for programs to either of the state's historic rivals, U of I and SIU. Nobody urged stand alone independence. Several downstate Democrats including Edley and Curran, who were hostile to the restructure, spoke favorably toward SSU's merger into the U of I (Fitzgerald 1993b). The campus itself was divided about the question, and the president assumed a neutral stance. "President Naomi Lynn said SSU has done well under the BOR, its current governing body, and could also do well as a part of the U of I. Taking sides could alienate either the U of I or the Board of Regents" (Pokorski 1993b). But regional legislators of both parties favored the merger. Feeling the larger plan would get stuck, some wanted the merger as a separate piece of legislation. Others, with stakes in the larger reshuffle, seemed resistant lest the smaller change force the larger issue.

Regional and racial concerns interacted with the restructuring proposal. Representative Arthur Turner, Democrat and a black caucus leader in the state House of Representatives from Chicago, argued that minorities are served mostly by Northeastern, Chicago State, and GSU and that their separation from downstate universities could hurt their future funding. According to Turner, the Chicago universities "may have trouble surviving on their own." Turner, not opposed to the SSU shift by itself, stated, "But if it's part of a larger deal, I say 'no'" (Fitzgerald 1993b). Meanwhile, there was word from Speaker Madigan's spokesperson: "So far, I don't think he is impressed with the arguments advanced in favor of any aspect of the reorganization."

In mid-April, the restructure bill passed the Senate 37 to 18, with votes that included eight Democrats, but opposition came mostly from Chicagoans. A separate bill, but part of the package, defeated the proposal to shift U of I trustees' selection from election to appointment. In the House, Democratic leaders, citing opposition from black legislators in the Democratic caucus, indicated the bill was not going anywhere. Meanwhile, any attempt to deal with the SSU merger was damned by faint praise from U of I President Ikenberry, and that made the Speaker cool to that particular proposal (Fitzgerald 1993a).

In early May, the restructure bill failed to get out of House committee. Only one Democrat, from Springfield, supported the proposal. Kustra blamed Speaker Madigan while expressing the hope that the matter would be negotiable for other considerations at the end of the session. According to reporter Doug Finke (1993):

"Governor Jim Edgar made reform of the university systems a major item he wanted approved this spring. Because of that, Madigan is reluctant to hand the governor a victory this early in the session."

On May 11, the *State Journal-Register* editorially asked Kustra for a compromise on the restructure to achieve the SSU–U of I merger: "There is no doubt in our minds that such a merger would be beneficial to both SSU and the U of I. We also believe that if lawmakers would consider the merger separately it would be approved." The same day, U of I President Ikenberry came to Springfield to say he was cool to the merger, that he was concerned about costs, that he would not support the idea unless it was part of the larger restructuring plan, and if it did happen as part of an overall restructuring, "we would not only accept [SSU], but we would make it a first-class institution" (Fitzgerald 1993c). State House reactions were that both the restructuring and the merger were dead for the session. Kustra criticized Ikenberry's "lack of leadership and vision" and suggested a move to combine SSU with SIU, the U of I's perennial rival.

There were other issues of prominence in the rest of the session—gambling boats for Chicago, firming up the budget, making the income tax surcharge permanent, enlarging the local government share of state income tax revenues. The House never did take up the restructure bill. The universities themselves became more preoccupied with the self-scrutiny called for by IBHE chair Art Quern's PQP. The task force agenda for higher education disappeared from view. However, SIU leaders came to Springfield after the legislative wrap up for a board meeting (Atkins 1993). Chancellor James M. Brown indicated that an SSU/SIU merger would work well and generate a variety of programmatic benefits while preserving campus autonomy. President Lynn of SSU dutifully noted that "we have no objection on going with SIU."

The political impasse did not change after the 1993 session or in the legislative session of 1994. The leaders on the campuses and in the legislature offered no changes of view, and no external events or players changed in a way that reshaped the political landscape. Restructuring higher education was off the agenda, and SSU remained under the BOR.

## Electoral Victory and Policy Change

What was important in 1994 was the electoral process. Edgar and Kustra would run for reelection. Democrats chose Dawn Clark Netsch and Penny Severns for the top of their ticket. Netsch's primary campaign committed her to a substantial income tax increase, and Edgar labeled her soft on crime. Meanwhile, President Clinton's approval ratings were low, and congressional Republicans were running an unprecedented nationalized campaign that was marked by a clear theme and message (Thurber 1995, 3). State Republicans were contesting for all available House seats, seeking to win the majority that they had expected to be the fruit of their reapportionment victory in 1991.

In October, an inconspicuous story was published in Bloomington-Normal by the *Pantagraph* (Thompson 1994). Both Kustra and Edgar had met with the paper's editorial board during the campaign period. The story opened with the following: "Elimination of the intermediary board governing Illinois State University remains a goal, but isn't likely unless Republicans take control of the Illinois House, Governor Jim Edgar said Tuesday." Edgar cited his desire to eliminate the boards since his days as a state legislator from Charleston during the 1970s. He blamed House Democrats for spiking the plan in 1993, saying change would be unlikely unless Republicans won a majority of the House seats in the upcoming legislative races. Kustra, for his part, indicated he wanted another blue ribbon task force to study the governance structure. Edgar confirmed his continuing conviction that there was still "an unnecessary level of bureaucracy" in higher education.

On November 8, 1994, Republicans won handily in Illinois. The Edgar-Kustra ticket won over Netsch and Severns by a 64 to 34 margin. Republicans claimed all the other statewide executive offices, picked up two of three U of I board seats, and brought thirteen freshmen members into the House for a majority margin of 64 to 54. They added one to their Senate majority for control by 33 to 26. For a comparable degree of Republican Party control in Illinois, one must look back to the 1950s and the era of Governor William Stratton.

By late December, stories began to circulate that higher education governance changes were actively under consideration (Hawthorne 1994). Representative Mike Weaver, Republican from Charleston, where EIU is located, prefiled a bill very much like the one in 1993, saying that "chances this time are much improved" (Allee 1994). In early January, Kustra was publicly predicting that the restructuring would happen soon, with SSU to be part of the U of I (Pokorski 1995d). The governor made the request in his state of the state address on January 11, and the next day, Kustra told the Bloomington newspaper that the elimination of the BOR and BOG was "a virtual reality" (Falcone 1995). He was quoted as saying: "The governor proposed a set of higher education reforms similar to those introduced two years ago. The only difference is we are part of a new majority." In addition, Kustra touted the shift from an elective to an appointive board for the U of I, which the governor also called for in his state of the state speech. Early legislator responses were favorable. Veteran Democratic senator Vince Demuzio joined central Illinois Republicans in saying he would support the SSU–U of I merger and would probably support the abolition of the BOR and BOG staffs (Williams 1995).

On February 1, minutes before a meeting of the Higher Education Committee of the House, a 429-page bill materialized. Besides dissolving the BOG and BOR, putting SSU into the U of I and establishing separate boards for the former system schools, it contained a provision making a single bargaining unit of the three campuses of the U of I. As a BOR school, SSU was, for purposes of a faculty union, a single bargaining unit. Faculty were organized by the University Professionals of Illinois and working under a collective bargaining contract that would remain in force until July 1, 1997. Ron Ettinger, spokesperson for the University Professionals of Illinois, realized: "It would put us out of business until we were able to organize the entire U of I faculty on all three campuses. There's no way we could do that in a hundred years." In short, Ettinger labeled the bill "a union buster for sure" (Pokorski 1995b). To be handled in a second bill was the matter of making the U of I board appointive.

The following week the Senate Higher Education Committee took up the bill. The faculty union opposed and so did several SSU faculty who were given the opportunity to testify. Also, Rod Groves, chancellor of the BOR, opposed, saying that the new structure would be an unbalanced one, making small schools compete individually with the U of I for funds. He warned that with seven new boards, competition for funding would cause a "feeding frenzy of lobbying" in the state House (Pokorski 1995c). Instead of testifying about the pros and the cons of the bill, Richard Wagner, IBHE executive director, loyally proposed to the committee a list of powers that Art Quern, IBHE board chair, wished to have added to the authority of the IBHE to coordinate all the state universities. Legislators passed the restructure bill on a partisan 5 to 4 vote, with the Republican chair, Senator Ralph Dunn of Carbondale, a reluctant supporter. The committee also approved the bill for an appointive board for the U of I, but nothing happened on the expansion of IBHE powers.

Before the end of the week, both bills passed the Senate. The restructure bill got 33 votes, while the appointive board bill squeaked by with only 30 votes (30 votes, a constitutional majority, is necessary for passage). Several Democrats, including Vince Demuzio, opposed the restructuring because of the bargaining unit provision (Finke and Pokorski 1995). On February 17, largely along partisan lines, the House passed both bills. On February 28, the governor signed both bills, happy to "reform and streamline" the system of systems and talking about a trailer bill to speed the merger of SSU with the U of I to July 1, 1995, and possibly adding to the authority of the IBHE. The time change would match with fiscal year appropriations and facilitate the transition (Pokorski 1995a), and that was adopted. The IBHE powers proposal was ignored.

In a curious aftermath story in Charleston, Republican Mike Weaver, House sponsor of the restructure bill, said that a notable local issue had a part in his effort. "The Chancellor's office [of the Board of Governors] provided me with a bit more motivation because of some of the things they did on Eastern's campus, particularly the way they treated Stan Rives" (Allee 1995). The story went on to summarize that Rives resigned in December 1991, after a year of controversy regarding hiring practices and a sexual harassment charge but that at a recognition dinner, Rives had called for a "revolution in the governance of higher education." The paper noted that "Governor Jim Edgar, who attended the Rives' dinner, delivered on Tuesday by signing a bill that eliminates the [Board of Governors] and the Board of Regents and creates local governing boards for seven of the universities, including Eastern. Rives said he was pleased." The piece also recalled that

Edgar, a Charleston native and Eastern alumnus, had himself sponsored an unsuccessful bill to restructure the state universities in 1979.

There were follow-up stories, particularly about the complexities of merging SSU with the U of I. The union did challenge the legality of the legislation changing the bargaining unit for SSU faculty, but to no avail. The transition for SSU was advanced to July 1, 1995, but the dissolution of the BOR and BOG and implementation of independent boards for the other seven schools did not take place until 1997. There was some conspicuous turnover of players. Stanley Ikenberry retired from the presidency of the U of I and was succeeded by an internal candidate, James Stukel, who came from the top position at the Chicago campus of the university. Thomas Wallace, president of ISU, who pressed for the breakup of the BOR, resigned after receiving unfavorable public attention for accepting salary supplements from the ISU foundation without the knowledge or permission of the BOR and its chancellor. Rod Groves, chancellor of the BOR, was ingloriously fired by his board, despite his earlier announced retirement. James Brown, interim head of the SIU system, retired and was replaced by Ted Sanders, a former state superintendent of education in Illinois, who had also served in the federal department of education. The proposal to enlarge the coordinative powers of the IBHE united nearly all the campus leaders in opposition, so no legislative action followed.

While the restructure legislation was a substantial change in higher education, certainly the biggest legislative enactment since the establishment of the IBHE in 1962, the House Republican leader considered it only a matter of secondary significance. Republican Speaker Lee Daniels claimed credit for what he called an "Illinois Agenda" that the state legislature had enacted in just nineteen days. In a letter published on March 12, he asserted: "After last week's business in the House, we have completed our 'fast track' agenda—almost a month ahead of schedule. This success is unprecedented in state history and I'm not aware of this level of comprehensive legislative achievement anywhere else at any time" (Daniels 1995a). Daniels listed tax caps for Cook County, crime bills, ending business restrictions, welfare reform, and education reform. He claimed partisan satisfaction as well as "triumph for all the people." But in the Speaker's estimation, the higher education restructure was not among the most significant accomplishments.

A later surprise to the session was a bill that passed the legislature to free the community college system and its board from coordination under the IBHE. That action would have substantially undermined the role of the IBHE with regard to the largest portion of undergraduate enrollment in the state. Governor Edgar vetoed the bill, and its sponsors were persuaded not to call for its override but to live with the unfolding governance processes of the state.

## Conclusion

In several respects, the story just told is unremarkable. State government and its institutions are big business. That business, in its many aspects, is conducted by democratically elected politicians. Sometimes differences among the policy specialists who operate portions of the government's business are appealed to the politicians. Other times politicians see fit to intrude upon the policy specialists and assign them new tasks, new organizational structures, and a different balance of responsibilities. In the matter of higher education policy, the latter example happened in Illinois, concluding in a major policy change enacted in 1995. But Illinois was not a special case. According to Charles Mahtesian (1995), policymakers in several states were bringing their state universities under closer scrutiny. The article title is instructive—"Higher Ed: The No-Longer-Sacred Cow."

What can we make of these changes? Is it an arbitrary outcome? A unique story? Alternatively, are there enduring patterns of policy-making that help to unravel and explain the political enactments that occurred? I am persuaded that there are explanatory theories that help one understand this policy story. More than that, the case reported here helps establish and further embroider upon those theoretical ideas. The next chapter spells out many of those theoretical ideas. The following four chapters put the higher education policy changes into theoretical context, enriching my understanding of what actually took place. A concluding chapter seeks to pull together my analysis.

# 2 | Policy Theory and Restructuring Higher Education

To analyze changes in the way Illinois governs its public universities, I find it helpful to reflect upon a few elemental ideas. The basic notion is that this is a study of policy, really public policy. Ripley and Franklin (1991) offer a simple definition for policy: "what the government says and does about matters it wishes to affect" (1). The relevant government in this case is state government, of course. Higher education is a state responsibility, and the states have organized in a variety of ways to manage and govern the different kinds of higher education institutions subject to their oversight. A recent study of major states by the California Higher Education Policy Center (Bowen et al. 1997) developed a typology of state governance systems, characterizing Illinois' as a federal system (other types were unified systems, confederated systems, and, the loosest arrangement, confederated institutions).

How does the government determine what policy will be put into effect regarding higher education? Not much theoretical guidance comes from the literature of higher education (see Lewis and Maruna 1996; however, for some preliminary categories, see Hartmark and Hines 1986; for some hypothesis testing, see Hearn and Griswold 1994). A recent national study of higher education changes (Marcus 1997) reported a mix of reasons for proposals in the states to restructure in the 1989–1995 period. Marcus noted, for example, that proposals from governors succeeded in two-thirds of cases (six of nine) compared to a 55 percent approval rate overall. However, a higher enactment rate (eight of ten) was achieved with proposals from statewide higher education authorities. Useful as the study is for categorizing changes, it offers little in the way of causal explanation for why most proposals succeeded and why efforts to achieve decentralization of governance were adopted as often as those to increase centralized control.

It seemed to me useful, therefore, to turn to works that examine the beginning stages of the public policy process. The first stage is getting policy ideas into the consideration mechanisms for policy-making. The second has to do with rendering those policy ideas into authoritative determinations. Whatever the form desired, there is a legitimating process. Is this to be done by law, by regulation, by reshaping tradition, by planning? As the case study has made apparent, the governance changes in Illinois were accomplished through the legislative process. So the theoretical guidance I chose to draw upon is that which focuses upon agenda setting and policy adoption. I turn next to John Kingdon, then Charles O. Jones, and lastly to Frank R. Baumgartner and Bryan D. Jones.

## Kingdon on Agendas and Alternatives

In a larger national study, John Kingdon (1984) asked a question relevant to this inquiry: How does an idea's time come? My interest is in policy ideas and the whys and hows of enactment. In an open political system, there are always a plethora of policy ideas being bandied about. Government, with its resources of constitutional authority and institutionalized power, can be the instrument to authorize and implement all sorts of such ideas. Why do public officials act on some proposals and address certain problems while ignoring others?

Kingdon fixed his attention on two broad, national policy areas—transportation and health. His attention focused upon two of four processes in public policy-making, namely, agenda setting and specifying policy alternatives. He largely ignored authoritative decision-making and policy implementation. He specified some terminology and derived a number of relationships to account for how and why governments do what they do in policy-making. The *agenda,* as he conceived it, "is the list of subjects or problems to which governmental officials, and people outside of government closely associated with those officials, are paying some serious attention at any given time" (3). He differentiated the *governmental* agenda, subjects getting attention, from the *decision* agenda, subjects actually up for determination (4). His inquiry considered how items move from outside of government into its web of relations through political representatives, policy elites including bureaucrats, and political changes wrought by elections (17). The processes for policy formation are three: problem recognition, policy generation, and politics (20).

The players who are important in getting items on the decision agenda are, as one might expect, the usual suspects. "No other single actor in the political system has quite the capability of the president to set agendas in given policy areas for all who deal with those policies" (25). The president is predominant because of his institutional resources (hire, fire, veto), organizational advantages (unitary decision-making), and command of public attention. The president's major appointees often play important parts in elevating issues. Staff are quite important, but are more significant in specifying policy alternatives than in setting the agenda. Likewise with civil servants, who are rarely "very important" but armed with longevity and expertise, they specify alternatives and shape implementation. In brief, then, with regard to agenda setting, "a top down model of the executive branch seems to be surprisingly accurate" (33).

Members of Congress too are highly important in agenda setting. "They are among the few actors in the political system who have marked impacts on both the agenda and the alternatives that are seriously considered" (38). Their legal authority, media visibility, politically flavored information, opportunities for policy entrepreneurship, and longevity make them significant but competing players. Congressional staff are rarely important in their own right in agenda setting, but "staff impact on the alternatives and on the specific provisions of legislative proposals is very great" (45). Indeed, with regard to the agenda, "to the extent that anybody is important, it is elected officials and their appointees" (47). The significance of interest groups is highly variable, dependent at least upon group resources, competition, issues, and electoral clout. They can often affect the governmental agenda by blocking items and by specifying alternatives. The media play a part in expanding conflict over an issue. Indeed, policy entrepreneurs may be able to "soften up" either the general public or specialized publics to proposals for policy change (64, 135) by gaining media coverage.

The mass media cover news rather than making it, and the popular attention to government issues corresponds to such coverage. Therefore, "media attention to an issue affects legislators' attention" (61) because they are media consumers and because media coverage affects their constituents. Media shape policy agendas because they are means of communication with a policy community, magnifying momentum by players, shaping public opinion, and sometimes focusing attention on outsiders.

Certainly elections can change policy agendas, and some policy matters are more likely targets than others. Shifts in partisan control of the chief executive or legislative chambers typically bring change to agendas and approaches to policy. Campaign promises and electoral coalitions shape the governing phase, but "there is nothing automatic about campaign pledges finding their way into public policy" (67). Kingdon distinguishes policy participants into two kinds: a visible cluster of elected politicians and appointed executives who set the agenda and the less conspicuous cluster of information specialists who generate alternatives.

Kingdon's genius was in separately analyzing problems and policy solutions. Using a garbage can metaphor, he argues that outcomes are "a function of the mix of garbage (problems, solutions, participants and the participants resources) in the can and how it is processed. . . . Solutions and problems have equal status as separate streams in the system" (91) and that events in the political stream occur independently of the problems and policy proposals. Although focusing events—crises, inventions, symbols—help in problem identification, "conditions become defined as problems when we come to believe we should do something about them" (115). Therefore, Kingdon infers that "the process of fixing attention on one problem rather than another is a central part of agenda setting" (121).

Key players are policy entrepreneurs, whose defining characteristic is "their willingness to invest their resources—time, energy, reputation, and sometimes money—in the hope of a future return" (129). Their return may come in response to any or all the incentives distinguished by James Q. Wilson (1973) as material, purposive, and solidary. Policy ideas that tend to endure are marked by technical feasibility, value acceptability, tolerable costs, anticipated public acquiescence, and the prospect of acceptability to legislators. According to Kingdon, "the chances for a problem to rise on the *decision* agenda are *dramatically* increased if a solution is attached" (150, Kingdon's emphasis). Through the clash of ideas and advocacy, numerous possible policy ideas are threshed into a "short list of proposals that are seriously considered" (151).

It is the politicians, those intimately involved in the partisan, electoral, and interest group fray, who engage in public debate, argumentation about merits, and acceptability of proposals, bargaining and recasting operational programmatic language and the formation of coalitions that determine policy enactments. Jurisdictional disputes may promote the acceptability of a policy proposal. Kingdon argues that "the complex of national mood and elections seems to create extremely powerful impacts on policy agendas, impacts capable of overwhelming the balance of organized forces" (171–72).

Having differentiated policy problems, policy proposals, and political stream, Kingdon characterizes policy advocates as waiting "in and around government with their solutions at hand, waiting for a development in the political stream they can use to their advantage" (173). He expects opportunities for advocates to open "policy windows" when the separate streams join and a small set of policy items is up for a decision by the relevant politicians. For example, Kingdon observes that "in 1965–66 . . . the fortuitous appearance of extra liberal Democratic seats in Congress brought about by the Goldwater debacle opened a window for the Johnson administration that resulted in the enactment of Medicare, Medicaid, the poverty program, aid to education, and all the other programs collected into Johnson's Great Society initiatives" (175).

The critical element for Kingdon in the decision agenda game is the policy entrepreneur. "Very important" or "somewhat important" in fifteen of twenty-three case studies, in only three were policy entrepreneurs "unimportant" (189). He notes that such an entrepreneur has a claim for a hearing, based on expertise, as a spokesperson for relevant others or as an authoritative decisionmaker. The entrepreneur can bring stakeholders into linkage and interaction. The entrepreneur will persist in the problem-solving effort.

This paradigm of policy-making is not neatly ordered. To the contrary, "alternatives must be advocated for a long period before a short-run opportunity presents itself on an agenda" (215). Yet there are patterns and regularities that are constrained by the political realities that determine which players exert what and how much political authority.

## Jones on Administrations and Their Agendas

Charles O. Jones (1995), an eminent scholar of presidents, Congress, and the policy process, acknowledges the conventional wisdom that obviously the president is setting the national policy agenda, but he notes that presidential participation and success do certainly vary over time and different circumstances. He seeks to understand the place of different, particularly recent, presidents in the complex process. He studies what presidents do in a larger context of what is going on in government and politics. He offers some differentiation for understanding agendas. By *agenda orientation* he means "broad trends in the role of government" (78) such as expansion of government role in domestic policy, consolidation, and contraction. Jones notes that these descriptors do not simply reflect partisan ups and downs. Regarding *agenda alternatives,* Jones agrees on the utility of Kingdon's usage of this terminology and his finding that presidents have more control over what is on the decision agenda than over the alternatives. But Jones finds that "presidents differ on the degree of control over alternatives" (79) and that this variation is subject to study and explanation. Finally, he argues that *agenda congruity,* "the extent of agreement among major policy makers in regard to agenda orientation and agenda alternatives" (79), is also a variable for which to account. He looks particularly at congruity between the president and Congress, expecting congruity to be not "1.0" but varying "between and within administrations" (80).

Jones looks at six administrations from Kennedy to Reagan, and at five successions. A couple of excerpts give the flavor of his findings. Of Lyndon Johnson he says:

> The evidence points to the fact that an agenda was already in place in 1964 when Lyndon Johnson gave it a name. Johnson helped facilitate the development of the agenda during the 1950s as Senate majority leader, but was by no means its creator. The assassination of Kennedy, the landslide election of 1964, and the continuity of congressional leadership contributed to a high degree of agenda continuity and thus support for programmatic alternatives offered by the Kennedy-Johnson administrations. In fact, it is likely that these events encouraged greater acquiescence to these alternatives than could have been expected had Kennedy completed his term. (84–85)

By contrast, "President Ford was in no position to propose a new agenda. He was very weak by all the Neustadtian measures of presidential power. His one principal source of power was that derived from comparing his political ethics with those of Nixon, and this advantage was compromised when he pardoned Nixon. Meanwhile, congressional Democrats had become considerably more assertive during the Nixon years, even to the point of proposing large-scale energy and economic programs" (88). But Jones also observed "considerable continuity of consolidative issues between the Nixon-Ford and Carter administrations—surely enough to question the extent to which President Carter set the agenda. Further, like Ford, Carter was unable fully to manage the alternatives. Agenda congruity was low even with a Democratic president and Congress. Whatever was sent to the Hill by the Carter White House often had to compete with proposals prepared by others" (93).

Of the Reagan administration, Jones observes that his election was interpreted as a stunning victory, perhaps "presaging a [partisan] realignment" (94). "The many changes in party and committee leadership in the House and Senate tended to reinforce President Reagan's control of policy alternatives for economic and budget issues" (95).

Jones makes the important point that presidents must cope with an existing agenda of items that carry over from a predecessor's administration. In addition, there is variable congruity between the executive and what others wish to do about either an existing or emerging agenda. What is clear is that presidents with high-agenda congruity have experienced high success in achieving policy victories. Jones describes a four-fold typology for understanding policy change by cross-classifying a "knowledge dimension" with an "intended change" dimension. This theoretical conceptualization builds upon an earlier typology set forth by Braybrooke and Lindblom (1963). As Jones indicates, the knowledge base for a policy may be substantial, objective, scientifically sound and verified, well reasoned, and carefully articulated. Or, by contrast, the knowledge base may be weak, vague, and based mainly upon intuited hunches. Regarding the intended change dimension, there may well be contrasting extremes. On the one hand, proposed change may amount to a grand new design. Proposals at the other end of the dimension merely call for small increments of change in the status quo.

Jones elaborates on all four quadrants of the typology, but the one of interest here is the one marked by low knowledge and grand designs. What might occasion proposals for change of this type? Jones observes: "This opportunity may come in the form of war or revolution but more typically in a democracy as the result of a crisis, massive expression of public opinion on some issue, or possibly a landslide election for one party. Whatever the cause, a policy breakthrough is achieved despite the limits of knowledge. In this instance the change is 'augmentative' if not actually quantum" (1977, 221). In his analysis of agendas, Jones observes: "Many of the achievements of the Johnson and Reagan administrations during the first few months fit into this fourth quadrant. Grand intentions were facilitated by an opportunity to act, even while acknowledging that the consequences of these actions were not known and that policy analytical capacities remained weak" (1995, 100). Most of the Johnson proposals for the war on poverty—model cities, upward bound community action, Medicaid, and Medicare—were highly speculative. So were Reagan's tax cuts, punitive interest rates, increased defense spending, and huge deficits.

## Baumgartner and Jones on Punctuated Equilibrium

What is striking to another pair of researchers, Baumgartner and Jones (1991, 1993), is the actuality of "punctuated change" in public policies. This theoretical idea has been used in critiques of evolutionary theory in biological studies (e.g., Eldredge and Gould 1972) and has been applied in several political analyses (Burnham 1991; Kelly 1994; Harris 1998; as well as Jones, Baumgartner, and True

1998). Baumgartner and Jones point out that public policies in a particular substantive area may remain more or less static for a long time, then undergoing rather substantial change, which itself remains enduringly in place. "Our primary thesis is that the American political system, built as it is on a conservative constitutional base designed to limit radical action, is nevertheless continually swept by policy change, change that alternates between incremental drift and rapid alterations of existing arrangements" (1993, 236). They commend Kingdon's notion that problems and policies are appropriately studied separately (5). They reflect at length about how and why policies can remain for long periods in a condition of incremental change, then giving way to abrupt and substantial change. They infer from both social choice theory and interest group–pluralism analyses that

> in any situation where voting matters, stability is dependent on the dimensions of conflict present, on the order in which decisions are made, on the number of alternatives considered at the same time, on how alternatives are paired if choices are made in sequence, on the number of voters taking part in the decision, and on a variety of other characteristics that are not related to or affected by the distribution of the preferences of those making the decisions. In such a situation, strategic entrepreneurs can manipulate the voting situation to achieve their objectives, even if they cannot change the preferences of those making the decision. Most importantly, any time political actors can introduce new dimensions of conflict, they can destabilize a previously stable situation. Since this often can be done, any stability is not necessarily indicative of equilibrium. (13–14)

They credit William H. Riker (1982) for this theoretical line of thinking. From pluralist theorists they derive the notion that elected politicians broker complex coalitions of interests that differ by issue areas. Moreover, because players vary in their political resources, those with great resources can sometimes underwrite periods of stability and maintain a policy monopoly. Yet their power varies over time, and competing interests at odds with one another can undermine even apparent stability, destroying the policy monopoly.

This theoretical thinking posits that "political systems are never in general equilibrium," so Baumgartner and Jones infer that apparent stability is sustained by "the existing structure of political institutions and the definition of the issues processed by those institutions" (15). There are numerous reasons adduced to say that these conditions can be durable. However, two dynamics can intervene. For one, "a change in issue definition can lead to destabilization and rapid change away from the old point of stability" (16). "Similarly a change in institutional rules, rules of standing or of jurisdiction can rupture an old equilibrium. If a social equilibrium is induced only by the structures that determine participation in its choice, then altering the structures (or changing the rules) can cause the equilibrium quickly to disappear" (16).

To understand the dynamics of policy maintenance and change, Baumgartner and Jones note some concepts. Policy image—how a policy is understood and discussed—shapes the way in which political operatives can define or attack a policy monopoly. "Policy images are always a mixture of empirical information and emotive appeals" (26). The information component may be complex and cumulative as scientific/technical/specialist data are gathered over time. Tone indicates the evaluative component, may be positive or negative, and can sometimes change very quickly. "That is, as the tone of stories in the mass media changes, say, from positive to negative, opponents of the policy have an opportunity to attack the existing policy arrangement" (26).

They also note the importance of policy venue—"the institutional locations where authoritative decisions are made concerning a given issue" (32). While some policies are regularly determined in particular venues, others are not. The very nature of American checks and balances is built upon the expectation that ambitious advocates may appeal a determination apparently decided in one venue over to another. The complexity of congressional politics has been increased by changes allowing multiple referral of bills and by procedures allowing committees to be bypassed (Sinclair 1997, 15, 54). So the possibilities for venue shopping and venue creation by American political players adds variation to the policy process.

Baumgartner and Jones build upon Schattschneider's (1960) notion about the importance of enlarging or restricting the scope of a conflict "to include or exclude those groups whom one can predict will be for or against one's position" (1993, 36). They also include insights from Cobb and Elder (1983) about "successive mobilization," as conflict expands "from specialists, to attention publics, to the informed public, and finally to the general public" (1993, 36). Adding to the notion of venue shopping, they characterize policy entrepreneurs as conflict expanders

> not limited only to appealing to wider and wider groups; rather, their strategies may be much more complex and specific. They may identify particular venues, such as congressional committees, state government organizations, courts, private businesses or any other relevant institution in their search for allies. In this process of searching for a more favorable venue for consideration of an issue, image manipulation is a key element. As issue expanders attempt to attract the attention of a new group of policy makers, they must explain why the issue is appropriate for consideration within that venue. So changes in image are used purposefully, in an effort to attract the attention of the members of a particular venue. (36)

Baumgartner and Jones pull together the theoretical threads of their argument by seeing an institutional framework that provides mostly stable policy-making. But policy entrepreneurs can destabilize the status quo by redefining policy images to appeal to otherwise acquiescent and apathetic members of the public. New participants can upset old policy monopolies, breaking down "what social choice theorists have called structure-induced equilibria" (38). The keys the policy players use are the interaction of policy images and the institutional venues for policy enactments.

## Summarizing the Theoretical Issues

Kingdon's major insight was to distinguish separate dynamics for problems, solutions, and politics. Did solutions predate the specification of a policy problem? Specifically Kingdon argued that "the chances for a problem to rise on the decision agenda are dramatically increased if a solution is attached" (150). While the top-down model worked, especially in the executive branch, and legislators also played substantial roles in controlling the decision agenda, how prominent are others in blocking agenda items and specifying alternatives? What is the impact of elections and partisan shifts? What are the consequences of media coverage? Who are the policy entrepreneurs, what is their investment, and what returns do they work for? Do the policy entrepreneurs wait for developments in the politics stream in order to bring solutions and problems together?

Charles O. Jones usefully differentiated the agenda orientation into which a new chief executive walks and the agenda congruity that such a leader may achieve or join. With Kingdon, he notes the relevance of others in specifying agenda alternatives. Also in Jones's typology of policy change, he suggests the sort of major policy shift of "grand intentions" in a context of low knowledge about the consequences of this action.

The team of Baumgartner and Jones discovered the pattern of policy change that alternates between incremental drift and rapid, major shifts of existing arrangements, what they call a punctuated equilibrium model. With their formulation in mind, I can look for new dimensions of conflict introduced to destabilize previously stable arrangements. Were there changes of issue definitions and policy image? Did the level of policy information change? Was the tone of the information switched from positive to negative, or the opposite? Were changes of policy venue sought or obtained? What efforts were there to change the scope of the conflict? Was there evidence of successive mobilization?

## Matters of Method

To answer these many questions, we turn next to the explanations and judgments of players in the policy process. Before doing so, however, let me return to the matter of methodology. When the Eighty-ninth General Assembly convened in January 1995, with Republicans in control of all the executive positions and majorities in both chambers of the legislature, I determined to directly observe proceedings. The issue most salient to me was the restructuring of university governance, particularly whether control of Sangamon State University would be removed for the regency system and be given over to the University of Illinois or

Southern Illinois University. I made it my purpose to attend relevant sessions of legislative committees and floor consideration of bills. As I indicated in chapter 1, thanks to my familiarity with many of the players who would take part in this policy change, I began a series of interviews. Between February and December 1995, I interviewed twenty-five people, all parties to the actions of this case.

**FROM THE LEGISLATURE:**
> Representative Barbara Currie, assistant Democratic minority leader
> Senator Vince Demuzio, assistant Democratic minority leader
> Senator Kirk Dillard, former chief of staff for Governor Edgar
> Chris Everson, Democratic staff to the House Higher Education Committee
> Representative Tom Ryder, deputy Republican majority leader
> Representative Art Turner, deputy Democratic minority leader and chair of the minority caucus
> Representative Mike Weaver, vice chair, House Higher Education Committee
> Representative David Wirsing, chair, House Higher Education Committee

**FROM THE EXECUTIVE BRANCH:**
> Bob Kustra, lieutenant governor
> Mike Lawrence, the governor's press secretary
> Tom Livingston, the governor's higher education staffer

**FROM THE EDUCATION COMMUNITY:**
> Phil Adams, legislative liaison for the Board of Regents
> Delores Cross, president, Chicago State University
> Garrett Deakin, legislative liaison for Southern Illinois University
> Ron Ettinger, lobbyist for the University Professionals of Illinois, a local of the Illinois and American Federation of Teachers
> Sam Gove, emeritus director of the Institute for Government and Public Affairs at the University of Illinois
> Rod Groves, chancellor of the Board of Regents system
> Ross Hodel, deputy director and liaison of the Illinois Board of Higher Education
> Stanley Ikenberry, president, University of Illinois
> Tom Lamont, elected member and chair of the board of trustees, University of Illinois
> John La Tourette, president, Northern Illinois University
> Thomas Layzell, chancellor, Board of Governors system
> Art Quern, chair, by gubernatorial appointment, of the Illinois Board of Higher Education
> Richard Wagner, executive director, Illinois Board of Higher Education
> Paula Wolff, president, Governors State University

In the analyses that follow, the interview data are my most important empirical basis for interpreting this case study. The quotations are longer than typical in political studies reports. This is to reflect fairly and thoroughly the nuances of explanation that the political and policy community players shared with me, doing so "on the record" and for attribution. In a few cases, the same quotation is repeated at a later location in the analysis to exemplify an additional theoretical point. I found the respondents to be generous with their insights and frank in their observations. Obviously and expectably, not everyone saw the same facts in the same way. Examples of those differences will be apparent. Yet, there is a great deal of consensus about what persons and forces were at work in this not atypical example of public policy-making.

# 3 | Problem Recognition and Policy Entrepreneurship

Having provided the recent historical context of higher education in Illinois and the theoretical milieu of policy change, I turn now to different perspectives on the restructure and the processes of change. I shall not attempt anything like a straight-line analysis. I will specify several theoretically relevant substantive questions about policy change. And I will draw upon the views of critically placed players in the policy process. From their perspectives, the meaning of what was taking place can be examined from several vantage points.

## Getting Restructure on the Agenda

Among policy specialists, the problem of Illinois' higher education governance was pretty much a nonissue. As recounted earlier, there have been occasional criticisms of the Illinois system of systems. The debate, stimulated by Albert Somit, former SIUC president near the end of the Thompson administration, was conducted almost entirely within the pages of *Illinois Issues*. The dialogue involved past and present educational administrators of that time. Somit made his sweeping criticisms, and others refuted him point for point. He proposed a restructure that was at best dismissed with faint praise and more evidently with wide disapproval. The debate was exclusively by the policy experts in the educational policy stream and did not engage the partisan political players.

After the debate in *Illinois Issues* was completed, the board of higher education took up the structure question in its more wide-ranging study of scope, structure, and productivity. The challenge to do the study came from the departing governor, James Thompson, but the challenge was given to the education establishment. The normal venue for such a policy problem was the Illinois Board of Higher Education. The IBHE created a study committee that, although it included legislative representation, was dominated by academics, and the chair was a previous IBHE executive director who had already published a refutation of Somit's concerns about structure in *Illinois Issues*. The IBHE committee provided nothing to the people in the political stream that would prompt any changes in governance. The dominant consensus in the education policy community was that higher education had other problems—especially slow budgetary growth. Educators believed that moving the structural furniture would burn a lot of energy and make divisive issues of turf protection visible without much substantive accomplishment. Then a top player in the political stream, Paula Wolff was at that time a key policy advisor to Governor Thompson. Asked whether she thought that the Thompson administration had, in fact, protected the system of systems from external pressure for change, she replied: "No, I don't think the Thompson administration protected the system of systems. I can't speak for the whole administration, but I was involved in all the reorganizations. The reorganization of higher education was a less significant priority than the other reorganizations that were undertaken. I think it just didn't have as much currency as some other reorganizations. I don't think there was an affirmative attempt to protect the existing system. I think it was just a less pressing need than some of the other things we did." So the governance of higher education was not conspicuous in the political stream, and the prevailing model was defended by a strong consensus in the education community.

Despite the overarching consensus supporting the system of systems, a festering issue endured within the Board of Regents system. The system was comprised of three schools (whose enrollments in 1991 are given): Northern Illinois University in DeKalb (24,895), Illinois State University in Normal (22,510), and Sangamon State University in Springfield (4,514). Both NIU and ISU had continuing ambitions to emulate the 1960s success of SIUC by becoming major independent universities. In fact, the regency system initially was only to include the two large schools, but when SSU was begun in 1969 and the IBHE prevented it from being a campus of the University of Illinois, SSU's governance was assigned by law to the same board as that over NIU and ISU. According to John La Tourette, the NIU president, the three institutions were unequally yoked. The two comprehensive universities and a small, specialized upper-level school "established a certain degree of instability in the system that existed during the next quarter of a century. At the same time, from the inception of the Board of Regents, you have ISU and Northern emerging on somewhat different paths. . . . The establishment of the BOR system was a good idea initially to bring two institutions up to a more mature status. If Sangamon State had not come into the system, it would have been a logical and anticipated outcome that the two large institutions would have become more like the U of I and probably justified their own boards of trustees at some point in time." The aspirations for separateness became endemic at NIU. Local legislators introduced bills for separate status, but they went nowhere in the legislature. It was a sore point for the regency leadership, who took symbolic steps to emphasize the regency identification over the names of the separate campuses. La Tourette notes, "in 1988 or 1989": "The board staff wanted us to have letterheads which would say, in bold letters, Regency System, and in much smaller letters below it, Northern Illinois University. Well, that just bombed like a lead balloon because the alumni and the public closely associated with the university said, 'It's Northern Illinois University! What is this thing, the Regency System?'"

Living with the conflicting aspirations made life at NIU difficult for campus administrators. According to La Tourette:

> I learned after I came here as provost, then as president, that this idea of having a separate board for Northern was deeply ingrained in the culture of the institution. One had to at least pay respect to it even if there was no opportunity to achieve it. What I mean by this is that it would be foolhardy for a president at NIU to neglect this sentiment that had built up over a long period of time and was very strong on campus. It had become part of the ethos of the university. It gave problems to all of the key administrators at NIU for a long period of time and frequently put them in a very difficult position. Local people expected the president to be an advocate for a separate board, and yet, the president was the person hired by the Board of Regents. I adopted a pat phrase: "I'm happy with my current board. If the legislature deems it appropriate that we have our own Board of Trustees, I will welcome them, too, but in the meantime I have to work with the Board of Regents." Essentially, this was the position taken by my predecessor, Dr. Monat, during his tenure as president. What happened here is there was such a basic groundswell over time that the issue of Northern having its own separate board assumed a life of its own, which transcended five presidents until my tenure.

Rod Groves observed the festering from the vantage point of the regency system. He had begun his career in Illinois as a member of the political science faculty at NIU in 1965, later joining the regents staff, succeeding to the chancellorship in 1986. He saw NIU and ISU as similar institutions that "persisted in thinking of themselves as different as night and day. They were pulled together in this artificial union [system] and instantly felt that this was a mechanism to control and impose restraint on them rather than a mechanism for their advocacy. Their efforts subsequent to that were in part to try to capture the Board of Regents but, in part, also to try to overthrow the whole structure. So they became a natural nexus for opposition to structure and for the advocacy of restructuring."

The president of the University of Illinois system, Stanley Ikenberry, could see and characterize the problem as a lack of community:

> It seemed to me, in the case of the Board of Regents, that there was a very significant problem of developing a sense of community within that system. The system needs to have some rationale, some sense of community that holds it together. And I think the Board of Regents increasingly, as years went by, seemed to have difficulty building that sense of cohesion. To a certain extent, but to a lesser degree, I think that was true also of the Board of Governors. But the sense of community, for example, in both of those systems, I think, is

very substantially less than the sense of community that one feels within the U of I. I think there is a sense of interdependence, if you will, joint destiny, between our two campuses in Chicago and Champaign. I'm not sure that Northern Illinois and Illinois State necessarily sensed that same sense of community.

The view by Thomas Layzell, the chancellor of the Board of Governors system, was not much different. Of his system and the Board of Regents system he said:

Partly I think they are less understood by the people than SIU or the U of I. Somehow they were viewed as different from SIU and the U of I; even though statutorily they were exactly the same, organizationally they were exactly the same. In people's minds, and in legislator's minds in particular, even the public's minds, they were viewed as being something different. Not a unity, not a single entity in the same way that SIU or the U of I. I spent a great deal of time pointing this out to people. The statutory powers were the same. They were organized the same with system and campus administration. That just didn't sink in with people. They weren't seen as the same.

La Tourette considered the Board of Regents system "a very, very loose system," and so was the Board of Governors:

It was always difficult for me to explain to someone in the legislature or an influential public citizen the fact that I didn't have the same power as, for instance, Stan Ikenberry, the president at the U of I. They would come to me and talk about the decisions that should be made relative to the university mission. In many cases, after reaching an understanding and an agreement, "yes we have to go in that direction," I would say: "Oh, by the way, I have to go through Springfield. I'm not dealing directly with a Board of Trustees where they will let me take the lead and present this issue." I have to say, "Well now, you have to understand a very complicated set of steps I will now have to go through if we are able to accomplish this objective that we have just talked about." In most cases, they would blink and have no understanding of what I was talking about, unless I explained it in great detail. I found that to be true with not only the informed public and what you would assume to be the informed members of the legislature but with people in much more responsible positions like the staff of the governor's office, the minority leader, or the majority leader of the House or other state officials. There was just no recognition in Springfield of the Board of Regents or the Board of Governors in the sense of understanding their meaning.

Change in the political stream in 1990 set the stage for change in policy. In 1990, Republican Jim Edgar was elected to succeed James Thompson as governor. Elected with Edgar as lieutenant governor was Bob Kustra, previously a representative and senator from suburban Chicago. There was no particular significance to higher education issues in the campaign. Edgar campaigned for law and order and fiscal integrity and argued the merits of making a previously adopted temporary income tax increase permanent. Edgar won a close contest, but Democrats retained majorities in the House and Senate.

An important early appointee of the new governor was Arthur Quern to be chair of the IBHE. Quern was on Edgar's transition team dealing with budget and state finances. He was a former chief of staff to Jim Thompson as governor. Edgar was then Thompson's legislative liaison. The two had worked closely on the same staff and knew each other well. In 1991, Quern was not interested in a full-time position in state government, having left in 1983 to go to the private sector in the commercial insurance business. However, with a background in higher education policy-making from his early career in the service of Nelson Rockefeller and a concern about bringing accountability and cutback management to state government, he accepted Edgar's appointment to the nonsalaried board chairpersonship.

Quern quickly brought board and board staff attention to the productivity aspect of the board's earlier committee report on scope, structure, and productivity. During the first year of his six-year term, he noted that "the various leaders of public higher education in the state started calling for [budgetary] increases that seemed absurd to me. They were talking about 12, 15, 18 percent increases, when everyone knew that the state had no money. And they were talking about it in a way I understood: you go and ask for an extraordinary number. Then you try to negotiate to an acceptable number. But I felt they were so far out of line with the reality of state finances that existed that they were eliminating themselves from the debate by asking for an exorbitant number." The result was that Quern initiated a distinctly anticonventional approach to higher education oversight. Dubbed PQP for the focus it put on priorities, quality, and productivity, by the fall of 1991, the universities were asked by the IBHE to make searching self-examinations. They were to report their strengths and weaknesses in 1992 and follow up in 1993, reporting the actions taken on the basis of such scrutiny. IBHE looked for universities to free up 6 to 8 percent of their resources for investment into "higher priorities" (Scobell 1993).

The initial response by some of the universities was to ignore PQP and hope it would go away. They underestimated Quern's insistence that they do self-scrutiny or subject themselves to tighter oversight. According to Quern:

> It was the initial absence of a positive response from the governing boards on this question of setting priorities and bringing people together to make some hard choices. The presidents and a number of the institutions were just doing and saying what they wanted. The governing boards seemed incapable or unwilling to deal with the way the campuses were approaching it. Lots of the campuses, or a number of the campuses, just started fighting PQP, saying all the data are bad or that the board has no right to get into this. At that point, I think that one of the triggering issues for me was if the governing boards were

not willing to use their power to eliminate programs, then I think the Board of Higher Education should have that power, and I'm willing to go to the governor and the General Assembly and ask for it. So I tried to create a situation where they had to step up to the plate and exercise the power that they had. That again focused on the governing boards and what their role was and what were they willing to do. Their initial response to PQP was very poor.

The poor initial response by some of the universities, particularly ISU from the regency system, evoked negative attention from the leading political figures, from Quern to the governor's office. It accentuated preexisting images that existed particularly in the mind of Governor Jim Edgar.

Political insiders and education policy players were well acquainted with Jim Edgar's political history. He was a graduate of Eastern Illinois University in 1968; in his senior year, he was student body president. His first opportunity for political experience was as a legislative intern on the staff of Russell Arrington, president pro tem of the state senate and legislative strongman of his time (e.g., see Pensoneau 1997, 84ff.). After eight years on staff, he was elected, in 1976, to the House, from the Charleston area, reelected in 1978, and took appointment as Governor Jim Thompson's legislative aide in 1979 and 1980. Thompson appointed him to secretary of state after Alan Dixon was elected to the Senate in 1980. Elected twice to that office, he succeeded to the governorship in 1991.

Mike Lawrence, Edgar's spokesperson and key aide, recalled Edgar's early interest in higher education restructuring: "The fact of the matter is that when the governor was a state legislator representing Charleston, he and [Springfield Democratic Representative] Doug Kane held a news conference back . . . before he became Thompson's director of legislative affairs. And at that news conference, they talked about reorganizing the system of systems. And, in particular, they talked about either eliminating the two governing boards or making them into one. I think there was also some discussion . . . at that time about SSU and about Southern and the U of I and some other things." Richard Wagner's recollection put Edgar's interest even earlier: "The governor has had a long-time interest in it. When he was a member of the General Assembly, he was involved in a task force reorganizing initiative with Representative Kane. I'm told that when he was student body president at Eastern in the 1960s, he had some questions about governance then. As student president, I'm told that he frequently did not have access to the president because the president was off somewhere meeting with the Board of Governors." The recollection that Edgar was a student body president and that later as a legislator he was interested in changing at least the Board of Governors was mentioned by members of the education community (Gove, Groves, La Tourette, Layzell, and Wolff) as well as those in the political stream (Adams, Currie, Deakin, Dillard, and Ryder). Adams, the long-time liaison for the regency system, who has known Edgar from his intern days, adds: "He's not a guy that's going to stand up in a meeting and say, 'I think I made a mistake.' . . . I don't think that he is the kind of person who's going to introduce a bill when he's a legislator and then think 15 years later, it's a bad idea."

The third political player interested in the organization of higher education was Lieutenant Governor Bob Kustra. With a master's degree in public administration from SIUC and a UIUC doctorate in political science, and previous staff and legislative experience, Kustra brought long and varied educational credentials into his public service. He had been a tenure track faculty member at Sangamon State in the 1970s. Over the years, he served in a variety of faculty capacities full-time or less at Loyola, Northwestern, Roosevelt, and UIC.

In Illinois, the lieutenant governor has few constitutional or statutory powers. Bob Kustra was recruited to the ticket by Edgar and, as a suburban legislator in the decade before 1990, offered some upstate balance to the Edgar candidacy. After the election, Kustra was assigned a variety of duties including that as an administrative advocate regarding education issues. Higher education policy became a topic of particular concern when Kustra had a speaking engagement in Macomb, home of Western Illinois University. Kustra's description to me is as follows:

> To be specific as to the real first moment when this idea emerged, I was at Western Illinois University. I was there to give a speech. That day, I met with faculty and administrators at Western, including the then president, Ralph Waggoner. I did some things in town. The day concluded at a dinner meeting of what I believe was some kind of economic development group that combined people from the university and the town. It's to get everybody reading off the same page for the future of the university in the town. I was the featured speaker. I sat at a table with the mayor. Throughout the day and into the evening, I had heard a variety of complaints about the interference of the Board of Governors into the day-to-day operations of the universities.

*Van Der Slik:* Is this Senator Kustra or Lieutenant Governor Kustra?

*Kustra:* I was lieutenant governor. I think this was in the spring of 1991. . . . I know we were in office. Because what happened is the next day this newspaper article runs that in my enthusiasm for the subject of giving Western its independence and giving Western Illinois more to say about what goes on in higher education, I called for the creation of independent boards of trustees. The minute I read it I realized that I had done something that I seldom if ever do in my relationship with the governor. As lieutenant governor, I felt like I had gotten a little bit out in front of him, that I had not checked in. I hadn't really thought of where I was going that 24 hours. I was really concerned, and I got right in to see him. I said, "I got over in Western yesterday and got carried away with what I thought was the solution to higher education and came up with this idea that we take all these universities under the Board of Regents and the Board of Governors and decentralize them and send the power back to the individual university boards of trustees." He looked at me and said, "I think that's a good idea. We ought to do it." And I put it to him in the form of a proposal. I said, "I do think the time has come that we do this. What do you think?" I think I caught the governor at an excellent moment. I think the governor was still smarting over the fact that the Board of Governors had been in this difficult situation with the president at Eastern. And the president at Eastern was very popular over in Charleston and on the campus. Many felt that he had not been treated properly and fairly by the chancellor and the Board of Governors.

Clearly the problem recognition step in this policy process took place in the minds of the elected politicians, but the inclination to engage in this kind of policy shift was formed in early adult experiences. Kustra speaks of his critical views of the Board of Regents and Board of Governors dating back to when "I was a faculty member on the lowest rung of the ladder . . . making what I would call close to a minimum wage at Sangamon State, [and] I saw them wasting $250,000 over at the Board of Governors on a public relations contract to create a logo for the Board of Governors." Kustra anchored his criticisms of the administrative organization to personal recollections of inefficiency and wastefulness. So the problem identification proceeded largely independently in the political stream, quite apart from the advocates and interested parties located in the community of education policy specialists.

## Focusing Events

Kingdon (1984) has called attention to the crisis or visible event that calls attention to a policy area and becomes a powerful symbol that "serves as an early warning" (103). There was no such event that had that kind of powerful meaning in the education policy community. The debate about university structure and governance that occurred during the late 1980s in the pages of *Illinois Issues* was remarkable only in the sense that the participants could not fasten attention on any particular crisis. A past campus president made his critique of the system of systems, but his fellow policy professionals simply rejected the criticisms in support of the status quo. No crisis added urgency to Somit's eloquence. Moving a governance agenda would have had little effect on higher education's perennial complaints—low salaries for faculty and rising tuition for students.

Because problem recognition was really in the political stream rather than in the policy stream, the search for focusing events should go there. Interviews with players in the process do reveal one for consideration: the firing of Stanley G. Rives from the presidency at EIU. Rives was a friend of Governor Edgar's. Charleston is Edgar's home town, and he is a conspicuous alumnus of the university. Rives was fired by the Board of Governors board and its chancellor, Thomas Layzell. During House committee hearings in 1993, Representative Mike Curran had challenged Bob Kustra, witness for the restructure bill, with the argument that breaking up the Board of Governors system was a tactic to pay back those who had fired the governor's friend.

Not surprisingly, different respondents saw the matter differently. The point is given some credence by those who were skeptical about or opposed to the restructuring. Rod Groves, chancellor of the regency system, saw it as a piece in the story of declining political support for the system of systems. Having taken an administrative position in the 1960s, then

> there was not anywhere near the kind of discontent with the whole system of systems that there has been in recent times. Of course, there are other things that go into it as well. You've had the change of the governor and the fact that Jim Edgar comes from a state university. He got his degree in a state university. He comes from a state university town, was an original detractor of the system of systems. As governor, he has certainly aided and abetted this cause. And then I think you have the incident of the estrangement and subsequent departure of President Rives from Eastern Illinois and the Board of Governors. Rives had close ties to Jim Edgar and committed himself more to the Edgar campaign than any other figure in Illinois higher education in the 1990 election.

If Groves thought of it as a precipitating event, not causal but relevant, his system's liaison, Phil Adams, bluntly thought it a major factor in why the BOR and BOG were vulnerable to political change:

> . . . I think the election, the combination of the election, [and] the situation that developed at Eastern two or three years ago.
> *Van Der Slik:* Firing Stan Rives?
> *Adams:* Uh huh, yes, his relationship and his wife's relationship to the governor and his wife, which was a personal relationship.

The lieutenant governor acknowledged the Rives factor:

> When I suggested this as a major initiative of our administration after my visit to Western, I think it's safe to say that the issue of Stan Rives had set in his [the governor's] mind that a problem existed in the way the Board of Governors was relating to individual presidents and campuses. When he heard this proposal, he felt that it fitted well with some of his concerns about higher education.

Though not a causal explanation, it's an element that crystallized the image of a structure in need of change. Representative Mike Weaver, legislative sponsor of the bill, representative of Charleston, and who had been a faculty member at EIU, saw the Rives matter in a nuanced fashion. Weaver was frustrated by the fact that in the normal course of affairs, the Board of Governors chancellor had put a

> prohibition on the [campus] presidents to not communicate with legislators. They were trotted out over here for appropriations. They were told to not speak unless spoken to. And that was the only contact that they were supposed to have with us [legislators], only under the observance of the chancellor. Stan

Rives is a remarkable individual. He's very stubborn, and he's very opinionated, but he had as his primary goal the health and welfare of Eastern Illinois University. And I really admired the man for that and his willingness to take that chance and speak out where he thought some comments should be made. But, as you know, the president serves at the pleasure of the chancellor's office without contract. And so they basically found some other areas that he had an Achilles heel on I guess and forced him into retirement.

*Van Der Slik:* People allude to his personal relationship with Governor Edgar. Do you see that playing into this whole story?

*Weaver:* No, that was one of the things that opponents brought up. Another was that when the governor announced he was running for office, that announcement was held at Eastern. Most of us thought that was a great thing, an important thing, because the governor was not only an alum of Eastern but also a former student body president. In a lot of our minds, it was very appropriate that his announcement to run for the highest office in the state come at that university. We thought it could only help to bring prestige and maybe a little bit of glory to Eastern. But the chancellor's office didn't quite see it that way.

Advocates for the governor were clear in their minds about the Rives matter. Senator Kirk Dillard, former Edgar chief of staff, was asked where the firing fitted into the story.

It does not. The governor sponsored a bill along with Representative Doug Kane from Springfield two decades ago to do essentially what this bill does. I think that this Stan Rives is just a red herring out there. I've met and talked to the governor privately about this. It is not Stan Rives that has driven this bill. It just is not. I've talked to him alone, just the two of us in private and socially. It's not Stan that has driven this bill. This has been the governor's belief since he attended Eastern Illinois University, was a student body president, and when he was a legislator from there.

For similar views, consider the governor's spokesperson, Mike Lawrence: "Well first of all, I know that some supporters of the status quo have said that the governor got a bee in his bonnet because of what happened to Stan Rives over at Eastern. Well, that's a nice, convenient argument for them except that it's contrary to history. The fact of the matter is that when the governor was a state legislator representing Charleston, he and Doug Kane held a news conference back in, I think it was just a month or two or several months, perhaps, before he became Thompson's director of legislative affairs." Later in the same interview, when I asked what else I needed to know about the politics of restructure, Lawrence returned to the Rives matter: "Well, first of all it's important to understand the history of it. Anybody who explains this as personal retaliation in behalf of Stan Rives doesn't know the real Jim Edgar. I would say this; he takes government very seriously. He's been in government all his adult life. So he wouldn't be screwing around with something like the higher education system. He will address himself to making the new organization work. Jim Edgar wouldn't do that."

Perhaps it is appropriate to give the last word on this matter to Thomas Layzell, chancellor of the BOG. He was a central figure in the Rives matter as one who Weaver believed unduly muzzled Rives and other presidents. Layzell was departing the dissolved chancellorship to head a higher education system in Mississippi when he spoke to me. He did not think that there was any single cause or precipitating event bringing the demise of the BOR and BOG. Asked specifically "about the Stan Rives incident," he replied: "Oh, I don't know. I don't think that played a major part in it. You probably can find people that will say differently, but I give the Governor more credit than that. He's been asked that a few times and has always denied it, and I think he and Bob [Kustra] probably believe this is a better thing to do. Whatever pique he or others may have thought about the Rives situation, I don't think that was a major motivator here."

The Rives matter was not a crisis. EIU was not materially changed because the continuing administrative hierarchy absorbed the loss. Nor were there a series of firings in the Board of Governors system or any other. No system breakdown occurred. It may have been, as Kustra noted, something that reinforced the governor's point of view, rounding out "preexisting perceptions," to use Kingdon's phrase (1984, 119). Perhaps the important point to make is that although it was less than a prompting event, it seems to have had the effect of adding to problem recognition for the player in the political stream most able to put the issue onto the decision agenda in the political system.

## Moving Restructure Along

Kingdon (1984) notes that a key part in policy-making is that of the *policy entrepreneurs,* whose defining characteristic is "their willingness to invest their resources—time, energy, reputation, and sometimes money—in the hope of a future return. That return might come to them in the form of policies of which they approve, satisfaction from participation, or even personal aggrandizement in the form of job security or career promotion" (129). Making policy happen is an affirmative activity. The political system of checks and balances is biased against change, particularly against substantial change. The legislative process is essentially an adversarial process, and two-party politics institutionalizes opposition to change. The entrepreneur, responding to material, policy, or solidary incentives, has to put forth conspicuous effort to change policy in the public arena.

The acknowledged entrepreneur in the policy action was Lieutenant Governor Bob Kustra. As stated earlier, he had appropriate qualifications—an undergraduate degree from a private college, a master's degree in public administration from SIUC, and a doctorate in political science from the UIUC. He began a tenure track position at Sangamon State in the early 1970s. During his ten-year legislative career, he had taught part-time in both public and private universities in the Chicagoland area. While in the legislature, he served on the higher education committees. The office of lieutenant governor gave him visibility statewide in a way that he had not before enjoyed. With a designation from the governor to be the administration's spokesperson on higher education reorganization, he had the staff, resource base, and license to make it happen.

After Governor Edgar mentioned his interest in disassembling the Board of Regents and Board of Governors systems in the 1992 state of the state and budget addresses, he named Kustra to cochair the Governor's Task Force on Higher Education. Kustra not only gave the task force its energy, but he was its public spokesperson. During the legislative process to follow, he was the most conspicuous witness for the legislation. After it failed in the legislature in 1993, he kept the idea alive so that when the political climate changed in November 1994, he talked the issue up again in the press, before the legislative session. He brought together the parties for the inclusion of SSU into the University of Illinois. He pressed the Senate Higher Education Committee chair to move the bill, contrary to the chair's own preferences. He saw the restructure through to adoption along with a companion bill to make the U of I board appointive rather than elected.

The acknowledgment of Kustra's entrepreneurial role came from several participants. Perhaps the biggest individual loser was Rod Groves, chancellor of the regency system. He affirmed that Kustra was a real player in this, not a front man: "Bob Kustra is the moving force. . . . Jim Edgar made him point man for education matters, and I think Bob has always been very much interested in higher education, and he was the moving force. No question in my mind." After the initial task force discussions about the shape of restructuring, it was Bob Kustra with whom President Ikenberry of the U of I corresponded to raise some concerns. When in 1995 the sticking point about SSU being made part of the U of I was the issue of the faculty bargaining unit, Ikenberry acknowledged: "Our staff did make recommendations to the staff of the lieutenant governor's office in terms of the language of the legislation. It was basically their legislation. And they were willing to address the issue." After the language in the bill actually changed the status of SSU as a bargaining unit, that provision could have been amended out of the act. However, no such amendment was allowed. According to Ikenberry, that was a determination by the governor and lieutenant governor: "It was their decision." The governor's spokesperson, Mike Lawrence, described Kustra as the governor's point person on the issue: "I think Bob's stake in the reorganization is that first of all he believes in it. He's warmed up to it a lot. Not that he was cool to it. But I don't think this was a major thing with him. He'd have to speak for himself. I may have the wrong impression here. My impression is that he really warmed up to it. The hearings were held, and the discussions were held. And he heard the rationale for keeping the system, and it didn't make sense to him. It's important to him that this gets through because he's invested a lot of time and energy in it." The governor's spokesperson saw this as having a potential political payoff. Kustra did, of course, run for the Republican Senate nomination, losing in the Republican primary in 1996.

The partisan implications were not lost on others. Phil Adams, the regency system liaison, who saw the publicity possibilities for Kustra, said:

> We all know that it is the lieutenant governor's job to kind of hang around and see if the governor dies. So, two or three years ago, Bob started talking about reorganization, I thought to get himself some publicity and get himself out of Springfield and certainly out of DuPage county, where he's certainly well known. This was something he picked up and ran with. It was good for him because he got on campuses, he got around the state. The campuses, with the exception of the three smaller guys up north [Chicago State University, Governors State, and Northeastern], are very Republican—they all have Republican senators, they have had for a long time. So, he was going to places where he was well-liked. They are spread out, so it gave him some good exposure. It let him carry this ball, instead of having the governor out there acting like he was just trying to help out his old buddy Stan Rives.

Similarly, Representative Art Turner, member of the opposition Democrats and the minority caucus, saw restructure clearly: "That was Kustra's deal. That was Kustra and Weaver. At least Weaver carried the banner in the house, but it was the two and Lieutenant Governor Kustra that was really out front leading this. This will be more that we'll probably hear about in a couple of years from now, in terms of his many accomplishments, as he prepares for future political endeavors. But I think it was primarily him."

On the Republican side, Representative Mike Weaver had been pushing restructure bills in previous sessions:

> It's been in the hopper a long, long time. Even before I got here. Northern Illinois University really was kind of a catalyst that started this. When he was in the House, John Countryman [legislator from DeKalb, 1983–1991] came to me when I was serving on the Higher Ed Committee and asked if I would support a bill to allow NIU to have its own board. And the more we got into the discussion of their situation, the more I realized that perhaps it could be of benefit to all of the schools, and we started investigating that further. Year after year, we had various problems with it. It would get killed for the most part for political reasons. Then we finally got it to a form that we thought we liked, and all of a sudden, the governor's office decided to put together the Higher Ed Task Force that Lieutenant Governor Kustra chaired. They came in after the report with some additional modifications that they wanted to see. And so we kind of had to change the bill after that. Well, pretty much everything that I was initially after really was encompassed in recommendations of the task force and in the bill. They went further than I did with some other proposals. One was a statewide committee to review those folks that wanted to be on these individual boards. And finally, after some discussion, we deleted that. No, I felt very comfortable in dealing not only with the lieutenant gov-

ernor and the members of that task force but also even some of the opponents when we got right down to it. They had some changes they wanted to make.

As an individual legislator's bill, this proposal could have been too broad and sweeping to come from someone with one medium-sized university in one system in his constituency. But the lieutenant governor could more legitimately address and advocate statewide systemic changes.

Kustra's reflections upon his part as entrepreneur came in response to my referring to him as point man:

*Van Der Slik:* Differentiating yourself from the governor, and you being the point man, what were your stakes in this? Did it have anything to do with getting you back on the ticket in '94? Is it a big plus for future electoral office?

*Kustra:* Number one, it had nothing to do with getting me back on the ticket. I didn't think about this at all during the months of the governor's bypass surgery, recuperation, and his asking me to come back. In my deciding to come back, I don't think I ever once gave this issue any thought. This was off the screen entirely in my life in 1994. I never thought, "Gee, if I get a Republican majority, we can come back to this." I mean it was really just off my screen. So no, I had not given this any thought at all. It certainly has been a plus for me I suppose in towns like Springfield, Macomb, and Charleston. People there really have chafed under the centralized and sometimes arrogant leadership from the Board of Regents and the Board of Governors. But I do keep in mind that 7 to 8 million people in the state of Illinois literally don't know this has happened, and they never will. The fact of the matter is that in the overall scheme of things, this is not equal to welfare reform. This is not property tax caps. So why did I do this? It has little if anything to do with my thinking about future office or some way to gain political capital. This is the fulfillment of years of working in higher education and being frustrated with the accumulation of arrogance in our administrators. The feeling that it's not right. We shouldn't allow administrators to accumulate wealth and power when students and faculty and taxpayers bear the burden of it. I will always feel that this was a great personal accomplishment for me. I felt the problem as an assistant professor at Sangamon State University looking way up the ladder. Now looking at the eventual action we've taken, it's a really good feeling to know that I was able to come back and rectify a situation that I think needed attention.

He minimizes the importance of material incentives, his future political possibilities, or accumulation of political capital. He emphasizes his fulfillment of a policy ambition.

## Conclusion

In the standard description of policy-making, the chief executive proposes and the legislature disposes. In this matter of higher education restructuring, we see the textbook model in action. In this chapter, however, I have been concerned to account for why the governor put this issue on the decision agenda. Clearly, it was not because the higher education policy community spoke with any united voice in favor of systemic change. Nor was there any clear breakdown in any system or the "system of systems." Particular university communities had separationist interests, and the most aggressive of those communities, NIU, was interested in a singular breakaway. The larger education establishment was content with the governance system, pursuing instead other concerns such as funding and changing educational technology.

In the lieutenant governor, the governor had a willing and able entrepreneur. Kustra's epiphany at WIU gave him a cause that enjoyed the full support of the governor, a cause that the governor had long before embraced when he was himself the representative of a small constituency. Now he had both the resources to advance a policy solution he long favored and a point man to give his preferred solution political legs.

The next chapter will address the matter of alternative specification. What were the alternatives to the governor's policy solution, and how would they be dealt with by and for the educators and the other political participants?

# 4 | Specifying and Defeating Policy Alternatives

The structure and processes of Illinois politics are democratic—open to the ideas, proposals, and demands of all kinds of people. The state's form of government reflects all the checks and balances espoused by Madisonian theory. Its professionalized bicameral legislature is fully equipped with staff and resources. Its members are quite capable of resisting the governor on the basis of their own political reading of what their constituents want as public policy. Two competitive political parties vie for control of elective offices in all three branches of government. Active in the Illinois political arena are hundreds of lobbyists who advocate for attentive constituents around the state (Everson and Gove 1993), not to mention the government-employed liaisons who speak for agencies of government, including the state universities. Scores of full-time journalists fill the statehouse pressroom and disseminate their stories through the print and electronic media around the state. The system is complex and richly nuanced, filled with positions and players who can engage competitively in the policy process. My discussion turns next to how policy alternatives to the governor's proposal were handled in the policy environment.

## Specifying Alternatives to the Restructure

The possible alternatives to the governor's proposal are innumerable. Let me note for example that the governor proposed to disaggregate two university systems, not all four. Seven campuses got their own governing boards, but the multiple campuses of the U of I and SIU did not. Sangamon State University did not get its own board like its partners from the Board of Regents. It was folded into the U of I system. The university most like SSU, Governors State, did get its independence and its own board. Even though the task force initially offered two organizational sketches for restructuring, its final report pushed only one model, which was eventually adopted. With all endless possibilities and variations, what actually occurred in the way of specifying alternatives? Because there were two cycles of activity, I begin with the action in 1993.

*1993*

During the first round of legislative consideration, the bill to restructure the universities was quietly adopted in the Republican dominated Senate. Republicans had their first majority in eighteen years. The bill was adopted with mostly Republican votes, but eight Democrats supported it as well. Opposing arguments were mostly by House members during committee consideration of the bill. The bill was hotly debated in the House Higher Education Committee. Several legislators, all Democrats, pressed the main spokesperson for the bill, Lieutenant Governor Kustra. The bill was not voted out of the committee. In short, legislative opponents were not for variations on the proposal. They preferred the status quo, and they had the votes in the House to prevent change from passing. As Kustra would later say: "The question Madigan [Democratic Speaker of the House] must have asked himself [was], 'Do I want the governor to get credit for this?' And his answer must have been 'No,' so he killed it. But I have never really believed that any Democrat who opposed this opposed it for some real or deep-seated philosophical reason. I think that the opposition was political, simply partisan." In later conversation, however, Kustra acknowledged the sincere concerns of minority caucus members and Madigan defending their interests:

> I don't know whether that concern is realistic, but since there was considerable concern and opposition expressed by some key members of the Black Caucus in the Illinois House, it's very possible that that is the reason why Madigan was operating as he did. The one thing I know about former Speaker Madigan is that he certainly didn't care about higher education. I mean especially public higher education. Mike Madigan cares about Loyola University, and when you get past Loyola University, he really isn't known as one who is going to stay awake at night worrying what happens to resources for public university education. So he was operating out of concern for his members. He always has to be concerned when a large number of them, like the Black Caucus, come to him and say, "This is not acceptable." I met with Senator Emil Jones two years ago, and I remember, specifically, he relayed the concerns of his fellow members of the Black Caucus: "If left alone, can Chicago State get the same resources it gets under the umbrella of the Board of Governors?"

*Van Der Slik:* And you did come back with your assurance to him that their current share would remain their share?

*Kustra:* Yes. Of course, I can't give an assurance, but what I can say is that I don't think there's anything in the passage of this legislation that affects the struggle for resources in higher education. This still leaves in place the way the Appropriations Committee operates, the way the Board of Higher Ed assembles the budgets for the individual institutions, and the way those budgets are then given to the Bureau of the Budget and the Governor's Office. The governor still makes his recommendation to the legislature. I mean the rest of the process is all intact. My argument all along has been that the Board of Regents and the Board of Governors as institutions were never the reason why Chicago State did well. I told Senator Jones what had most to do with Chicago State doing well is his and his colleagues in the Black Caucus raising holy heck any time there was any problem with that budget. They are not going to go away. So I'm confident that Chicago State will be able to survive and prosper under this system, assuming that they leverage the same kind of political control they've had in the past.

Meanwhile, most of the higher education establishments were content with the continuation of the system of systems, although presidents at some BOR and BOG schools were agitating surreptitiously for separate existence. The process of policy change was simply halted by legislative defeat in the House. It was not accompanied by alternative policy specification.

### 1995

In 1995, there was little in the way of alternative policy specification. Early in the session, Republicans offered a bill, actually a 430-page amendment, to a vehicle bill that had already been assigned to the House Higher Education Committee. In just a matter of days, the bill passed without further changes, having actually been heard in committees and on the floor of both chambers of the legislature. The governor promptly signed the bill into law, completing the most sweeping changes in higher education in the state since the establishment of the IBHE in 1961.

## Heading Off Alternatives

If what Kingdon has described is the normal policy process and the chief executive puts a major item on the decision agenda, the specification of policy alternatives by any of a variety of players is the expectable response. However, that phenomenon was notably absent in the policy environment in which the Illinois higher education restructure was considered. In 1993, the opponents beat the proposal; in 1995, the proposal was adopted in whole cloth. What inhibited the specification of alternatives? There seems to me to be at least four aspects to the explanation.

### Solving the SSU/Union Problem

In the 1993 process, the most prominent of the higher education players was Stanley Ikenberry, president of the U of I. He never pressed for the restructure proposal despite the fact (because of the fact?) that it made Sangamon State a campus of the University of Illinois. His resistance was not conspicuous, but he made his reluctance obvious to the governor and legislative players. Ikenberry's description of 1993 was to say of the governor's reorganization plan: "I don't think that it was among our top priorities. . . . I don't think we were pushing very strongly in one direction or another. . . . We sensed that probably the reorganization at that time was not likely to be successful." Ikenberry was in dialogue with Kustra about the proposal regarding the task force report:

> I had some correspondence with Bob Kustra at that time, in which I raised some concerns about the proposal. First, I was not convinced at that time that a rational case had been made to reorganize higher education in the state. It wasn't clear to me that there was any obvious rationale or purpose underlying the various recommendations. And I was concerned at that time that it might lead to undue fragmentation within the higher education system. And I did register those concerns. I think as I continued to work with it, while I continued to have many of those concerns, it also seemed to me that the rationale behind the reorganization became clear. Namely, that people did honestly feel, from a philosophical standpoint, that moving the governance and the decision making closer to the campuses for many of these state universities would be a step forward. It would help reduce the bureaucracy, that it would give better oversight and perhaps better advocacy to the individual campuses.

For Kustra, the policy entrepreneur, following an auspicious beginning the late spring of 1993, this was a frustrating time. House Democrats had tied the bill up in committee. Art Turner, a Democratic Party leader and spokesperson for the minority caucus, was convinced that the two schools serving the highest proportions of minority college students in Chicago were best served by being a part of a system:

> One thing that I did know was that the schools who were under the BOG, particularly those schools in the city of Chicago, I thought they stood a fighting chance because of that relationship and nature of being hooked up with downstate schools. So I was adamantly opposed to breaking up the Board of Governors. Even as we will discuss the issue this year, we're still opposed to that change in structure. I think what it's going to do is polarize higher ed in the state. I think schools like Chicago State and Northeastern, regardless of how strong their boards are, will suffer until there is some change in the corporate community in the city of Chicago. Those schools could be left high and dry. I also was concerned about the affirmative action goals that had been established through the system of systems. Long term programs had been designed to deal with this question of recruitment and retention of both minority students and faculty. No one has said where that goes from here.

For Kustra, the best kind of help would have to come from the state's most prominent leader, Ikenberry. Instead, Ikenberry was reluctant. According to Kustra:

> Someone asked me in committee the other day if the U of I orchestrated this, and I laughed. I said: "Orchestrated it. They didn't really want it." I mean from

the beginning there was a relatively well known reluctance on the part of the president of the University of Illinois to really jump in and take any leadership. I think he was concerned about the issue that ended up getting into the last few weeks of this thing, the issue over the unionization of the Sangamon State faculty. He didn't quite share that with us two years ago. Then I couldn't understand why the president of the flagship university of the state of Illinois did not want to have his university's presence in the capital city. The overwhelming majority of states in this country have the presence of a major university in the capital city. The fact is he didn't want it. I think SIU was going along like a good team player. I think SIU's leadership, the chairman and the members of the board and the presidents, felt like, "Well, we don't want to rock the boat. The governor and the lieutenant governor seem to have their eyes set on U of I as the likely partner, so we won't get in the way." There were some moments when I became so frustrated over the inability to get the U of I more excited about this initiative that I even said publicly and privately that if the U of I didn't want to do this, then we should talk to SIU, because I think it was clearly in the best interest of Sangamon State to get linked up with one of these two schools. As you know, I always joked about the fact that I'm the perfect guy to bring the subject up because I can't be accused of having a bias or a conflict of interest with my SIU degree and my U of I degree.

Was the association of SSU with SIU ever a real option? Apparently, only before the 1993 bill was introduced. According to Garrett Deakin, liaison for SIU:

> We took this issue seriously. We looked at it. Some board members looked at it, as did the president and the chancellor. They thought it was worth exploring. People aligned with SIU talked to the governor and talked to the lieutenant governor over this, this is back in '92, '93—before the gov made his selection with SSU and the U of I. At that point in time, back in '92 and '93, there were behind-the-scenes discussions. Some paperwork did go forward that showed some pluses for the SIU/SSU merger. But the decision there was to go the public affairs route. Once that decision was made—
>
> *Van Der Slik:* Who made that decision?
>
> *Deakin:* That was the governor. Once that was made, it made it very, very difficult two years later to change some minds. Now, it didn't mean that we didn't try.... [But the problem] went back to '92, '93. We felt very comfortable. They at least gave us the chance, the choice, the opportunity to vie for SSU. We took a shot. We didn't have a whole lot of time. It wasn't like you had six months, or anything like that. It was just a matter of a week, ten days, two weeks; it wasn't much time to put something together and send it up to them, and then try and convince them to go with SIU. Back then, that wasn't a problem. Once they had made their decision, once they had publicly said where they were, then that made it very difficult to overcome.

After that, Deakin did not consider the prospect of SSU going to SIU of any likely feasibility. It was not changeable through lobbying. Others, such as Rod Groves, chancellor of the Board of Regents, acknowledged Kustra's preference. Kustra's argument was that the public affairs university fit better with the U of I than SIUC, and Kustra had the public affairs credentials to make that case. When the U of I was reluctant, "Kustra used SIU more as a pawn than a real option, a real alternative. It was a way of squeezing a somewhat reluctant participant in Champaign-Urbana," according to Groves. Ikenberry understood the matter similarly. Whether or not to accept SSU into the U of I was a substantial decision within the U of I system. According to Ikenberry: "I think so long as the University of Illinois was prepared to accept Sangamon State, I think that SIU was not a serious rival. I think if the U of I had rejected the offer, then I think that for Sangamon State, SIU would have been the successor apparent."

The U of I had to decide on the acceptability of SSU. According to outsiders like Thomas Layzell, chancellor of the Board of Governors: "My understanding through the higher ed rumor mill is that there were really some pretty serious internal battles among the U of I and the U of I central administration about whether or not this was a good idea for them. In some ways, it is a terrible mismatch. I'm not denigrating Sangamon. It is just you've got a major research graduate level institution, and that certainly is not what Sangamon was created to be. And I think Sangamon will now become something other than what it was created to be. Just inevitably." Layzell and others in the education community recognized that U of I central administration would have great difficulty melding dissimilar campus educational cultures into an integrated single system.

The debate within the U of I was acknowledged by Tom Lamont, U of I board chair in 1992 and 1995. In the 1992–1993 round, he described Ikenberry's interest:

> I think Stan shared an interest in coming over here [obtaining a Springfield campus]. But he also weighed it with the advice and counsel of his immediate staff, who were not 100 percent in agreement with that. In fact, there were differences of opinion within central administration. Strong differences. Each side of which could articulate well the reasons why it should or should not happen. So I think he became somewhat ambivalent about it, particularly when Madigan was reluctant. But the new chancellor at Urbana, Michael Aiken was interested in it. . . . He was new to campus within a year when this conversation came up. He felt something should happen under the Ikenberry tenure, because Ikenberry was probably the only one strong enough to push it. So he and I had discussions on it; we never truly initiated movement. The movement was independently raised here in Springfield.

Eventually, Ikenberry and the board came to a judgment about support for the governor's package. Ikenberry observed: "I think that the strongest support, the change supported by near unanimity seemed to be for the transfer of SSU to the

U of I. Second was the creation of independent governing boards for the other university campuses across the state. And I think the third-ranking issue in terms of consensus of the need to change related to the U of I Board of Trustees. I think there were some who believed that the legislature might not act on that issue." Still there was a significant problem regarding SSU:

> Our major concern, as it related to Sangamon State, a major concern, was the fact that SSU had a unionized faculty. U of I, two campuses, were not. Ordinarily, this might not have been such a significant issue, except in the case of SSU and its relatively small size. Also. . . I think it will inevitably have [problems] in gaining stature and respect over a period of time within the U of I family. It seemed to me that it simply wasn't wise to set up a condition in which there would, from the very beginning, be two separate classes of faculty. If that were to take place, it seemed to me that would put Sangamon State, and the campus' development, behind the 8-ball in the beginning. It will be an uphill struggle, anyway. So, it wasn't necessarily a price—I don't think it was ever put in those terms—but we did recommend a solution to that issue. And we're pleased that it received as much support as it did.

Lamont acknowledged the faculty concerns about SSU's union, although he himself, elected to the board as a Democrat, had sympathy for the faculty union at SSU:

*Van Der Slik:* What concerns did the board hear from the two campuses about any or all of this or particularly the SSU part?

*Lamont:* Again, we heard it in the information coming right from Stan Ikenberry and our board secretary. The general consensus among faculty is that faculty and governance of the university should be handled better through a faculty senate and not through a labor organization. That was the traditional way that it had always been done on those two campuses, and I think they felt that was the way it should continue. Personally, I am not so sure many of the board members necessarily shared some of that concern. We are not on campus, and I don't know the culture. I didn't particularly see how a hundred and sixty members of a faculty union significantly removed from the other two campuses could have a real impact, other than make it somewhat awkward in how we handle things. I personally do not see that it is the end of the world—I hate to use that phrase—as significant as others.

*Van Der Slik:* So there was a visible concern by the campuses.

*Lamont:* At least that was what was communicated to us by the administration. We had faculty senate people who attend our meetings—called observers. The administration spoke in their behalf. They did not speak formally nor do they ever. But I think there was general consensus.

*Van Der Slik:* We don't need this.

*Lamont:* No. It was more than we don't need it—we don't want it.

Getting Ikenberry on board required the initiative of the Edgar administration. The governor's higher education staffer Tom Livingston's view of the 1995 legislation emphasized the union issue:

The most important provision of that was the teachers' and professors' union provision that they would be a part of the entire system. We were told that the university administration would be pretty neutral which in essence in this case would have been non-support.

*Van Der Slik:* "They" being the U of I?

*Livingston:* The President's office. It was one of their strongest concerns regarding this legislation. We went back and forth on that internally here and made that decision. Then it was full speed ahead on that merger from their end.

*Van Der Slik:* So they accepted it under the circumstance that you would handle that problem?

*Livingston:* Yes. That was "the" problem from their end. The Governor's position was—he wanted to know from a historical perspective how systems handled this—we called around to some other states; we didn't have a lot of examples across the border—and also discussed when Chicago was formed.

*Van Der Slik:* U of I Chicago?

*Livingston:* Yes, U of I Chicago. Then, based on those investigations, it was decided that this would be the best time to do this, right up front. If SSU was to be part of the system, it would have to go in under that provision. A lot of the UPI [University Professionals of Illinois] labor folks said, "We're not against the merger; we are against this provision that is a part of the merger." So even they weren't opposing the actual merger. They certainly didn't like this and still don't like this part of it. I think the Governor said, "If there is anyway we can try to work with them along the way that is fine; but on this very basic point we would side with the University."

The task of preparing the legislation fell to the lieutenant governor's staff. Representative David Wirsing was chair of the House Higher Education Committee, where the bill first publicly surfaced. While most of the content of the basic bill was well known, the new wrinkle was the provision that amended the Illinois Education Labor Relations Act. The new language specified that all campuses of the University of Illinois would be a single bargaining unit. According to Wirsing: "I didn't have any personal input into that aspect of the legislation. So the larger energy came from the governor's and the lieutenant governor's office and as well from my leadership's office [Speaker Daniels] as well. They decided how to deal with that."

The labor relations provision was a surprise. According to Chris Everson, the Democratic committee staffer for the House Higher Education Committee:

We did not see the amendment until five minutes before committee convened, but as happens in the capitol, people had heard things. A senator had called my spokesperson of the committee, Representative Judy Erwin, and said, "We don't think there are a lot of changes in this bill, but work from the back of the bill and see if you can find some labor language about Sangamon State," and so we did. In a 430-page amendment, we started in committee, and our guys were yelling at them because they violated their own rules about giving amendments 24 hours in advance. So everybody is yelling and we're kind of frantically looking, and we found the labor lines and started asking about it.

Chair Wirsing disagreed about any rule breaking. The bill, actually an amendment to a vehicle bill, was dealt with at the second regular meeting of the legislative session. At the previous meeting, Wirsing, as the new chair, had discussed with the members how he would lead the committee. His practice would be not to create subcommittees for handling amendments:

> Everybody thought that was a good idea. So I also said that if there are amendments being presented, it would seem appropriate that they were presented in a timely manner so that the staff on both sides would have the opportunity to at least go through the amendments and we could debate in committee with some level of understanding of how the amendment changed the underlying bill. We actually had adjourned, and then my counterpart from the Democrat side said, "What's the time limit on how soon prior to committee that these amendments have to be to the committee?" I thought I had stated we were adults; we ought to be able to work this out. So somebody on the minority side said, "What about twenty-four hours?" I said, "That's fine." So, we didn't vote on it. Actually, we were in adjournment, so it wasn't an official committee action. But I thought it was a good guideline. The next Monday, I get a call in the district office from the governor's office saying the governor wants the U of I Trustee bill and governance bill to go on fast track. So in order to accomplish that process, we had to bring it to the committee on Wednesday of that week. While that governance bill was a fairly large bill, I forget now, 400 and some odd pages, and each committee member is to have that amendment in front of them, well, that is a lot of copying. My higher education staffer pulled the amendment together and went to the legislative printing unit, and ultimately we got that amendment 10 minutes before the committee meeting started on Wednesday at 4:30. So I took all kinds of harassing rhetoric from the other side that I had broken my own rule and so on and so forth. But we did pass it on through. And it was a non-partisan bill.

The union perspective on this step comes from Ron Ettinger, lobbyist for the University Professionals of Illinois, a local of the Illinois and American Federation of Teachers, and also a Sangamon State University faculty member. He was present to indicate his opposition to the basic restructure bill. He expected it to pass easily and was not going to waste his breath in opposition:

But we kind of leafed through this rather thick document as we were sitting there waiting for the hearing to start and discovered the awful reality that the SSU group was going to be essentially eliminated. And that's when I filed a slip that I wanted to testify. It's an interesting thing. At the time we were reading it and trying to make sense out of it. When you first read something you don't know for sure what it is. Everybody that we talked to figured, yeah, I think your interpretation is right. I think they're out to get you. When I testified on the bill, I asked the representatives gathered if they could help me with the interpretations. And no one responded. I actually read that portion of the bill—it's not that long; it's a paragraph—and announced to them that I wasn't an attorney, but as I read it, it looked as if they were creating one giant bargaining unit and that this would essentially put our union out of business as far as representing SSU faculty. Not a person on that committee, including the chair, responded. My guess is that they hadn't seen it either.

*Van Der Slik:* And so you clearly understand that language was prepared elsewhere and dropped into the bill.

*Ettinger:* Yes. That language was prepared at a time and place that none of us knows at this point. But we had seen the bill, the previous bill, many, many times. And that's, I think, why this jumped out at us, because it was something that had never been in there before, as far as I know, never discussed anywhere, in any public forum. It caught us by surprise.

Although as much opposed to the basic legislation as Ettinger, Rod Groves characterized Ettinger's circumstance as an embarrassing one:

> I think that Ron Ettinger was caught with his pants down. His friend Bob Kustra had convinced him that it was just going to be fine. There wouldn't be any problems in this regard. Don't worry about it. He reads the language and he says, "How in the hell did that happen to me?" I think that he was just absolutely caught with his pants down. I think other union leaders at Sangamon were the same.

Ettinger did not give up at that point. He received assurances that more conspicuous union leaders would defend the SSU bargaining unit. Support would come from Don Johnson, Illinois president of the AFL-CIO. According to Ettinger, sympathetic concern came from unexpected places: "People who had absolutely no reason to want to support our little union were coming up and offering help, including some Republicans who were working with us. . . . I will just tell you that some high ranking Republicans made sure we got into the inner circles. We had nice chats with [Speaker] Lee Daniels, the leadership on the house side." However, the crucial meeting was in the lieutenant governor's office:

*Ettinger:* We had one rather lengthy meeting with the Lieutenant Governor, who was representing the Governor because he was gone. We thought it was just going to be an exclusive meeting—his staff and the unions. But he invited Stan Ikenberry; he came in late, and what Kustra did was interesting. I don't know if you've been to his office, but he's got a kind of conference table extension from his desk. He sat at the desk, and the union representatives were on one side, and Stan Ikenberry and his lobbyists and some of his staffers were on the other side. Bob introduced us and said, "Well, I'm going to try and mediate this fight." Well, we thought the fight was between us and Kustra. He rather quickly turned it into a fight between us and Stan Ikenberry. It was a cordial meeting. I think that we got all of the issues out on the table. I felt pretty good right up to the bitter end. People were smiling and nodding their heads. I thought that we pretty well convinced them that we should do something different, and then Bob Kustra says to Stan Ikenberry, "Well Stan, what you're saying then is that you won't accept Sangamon State unless we have this clause in here that does away with their union." And Ikenberry, of course, is as smooth as can be, so he said, "I certainly wouldn't put it that way Bob." So he put it in his own words, which sounded much easier to take. But essentially that's what the bottom line was, "No, I will not take SSU. I will not take this thing you're imposing on me unless you give me these things. One of which was, we want that place to be without a union." And I think another was a commitment that I've only heard about, certainly not in this setting but in others, that he wanted a $2 million bump in his budget, in order to take care of any responsibilities associated with SSU. And I don't know what else. In fact, those were the two big things. Get rid of that union and give me some cash. Why Stan ended up having to play the hard guy, I haven't figured it out yet. I really haven't. I don't know if it really was his initiative or if this was just a game that they were playing because he's leaving anyway. Why not use him as the fall guy?

*Van Der Slik:* But you did have the impression that he received SSU reluctantly at best, and only without a union.

*Ettinger:* He made that very clear. He told the lieutenant governor early on, "Look this was not my idea. I didn't want this in the first place."

*Van Der Slik:* Did the lieutenant governor claim the idea at that point?

*Ettinger:* Yes, he did. He said, "I admit, I am the father of this." It sounded—it wasn't real convincing to me. It sounded as if this had been worked out in advance. This was the hard-guy/soft-guy routine that they were doing for our benefit, because it doesn't jibe with other things I've heard. I understand that the U of I has wanted desperately to have an operation in Springfield, for decades. That wish was no weaker this year than in past years. I think he may have gotten himself into a good negotiating position by saying, "Oh no, I don't want that. But, I'll take it if you give me this." Stan, as usual, scored on this. He's got a lot of clout down there. I've never seen him control something quite this huge. But I have seen the U of I do well over the years, even when you wouldn't expect it.

For his part, Ikenberry described the same meeting as "substantive," "an honest exchange of views." That there was never a vote on an amendment to remove the bargaining unit language was the administration's call—"their decision."

Procedurally, the most favorable venue for defeating the bill was in the Senate Higher Education Committee. The union issue was no longer a surprise. The chair of the committee was the venerable Ralph Dunn, from southern Illinois, who believed that the best interests of SIUC would not be served by the U of I having a campus in the state capital. The nine-member committee had four Democrats and five Republicans. Dunn told Ettinger he would not vote the bill out. According to Ettinger:

> Now he said that in the presence of a number of people, including the SIU folks, who for their own reasons didn't want this to happen. Then, during the hearing, and we had been there for two or three hours worth of testimony, we could see the governor's people occasionally going up and whispering in Dunn's ear. Frank Watson, at one point, spent a lot of time kneeling next to Dunn and talking to him. Who knows what they said. But by the end of that hearing, Ralph Dunn said, "Well, sometimes you have to be a good soldier." The vote was already tied at four–four. It was time for him to vote. He said, "Therefore I vote aye." On the way out of committee, he said that this was one of the worst things that he's ever done, going against prior commitments and going against his better judgment, and he vowed that he wouldn't vote for it on the floor.

According to Senator Kirk Dillard, the Senate Republican sponsor of the bill, Dunn was reminded that SIU has a medical school in Springfield to defend, and although some in the U of I might also want to take that over, "he's received a lot of assurances that that will not happen nor should it happen." Who really did the pushing for the administrative bill? According to Dillard:

> I think if Ralph could have done it, had his druthers, he would have wanted SIU to control Sangamon State University in general. But the community here in Springfield, and I think they're right, the business leaders and civic leaders, wanted Sangamon State to be part of the University of Illinois. In the end I think the community here in central Illinois won out. And SIU is a great institution, but if I were at Sangamon State, I would rather be part of *the* University of Illinois, a major land grant university, as opposed to SIU. That's not a cut on SIU. It's just a fact that I would rather be part of the major university of the state.

*Van Der Slik:* Who did you have to work on to uphold, and who really did the pushing or the pressure?

*Dillard:* The lieutenant governor spoke to Senator Dunn and, I think, convinced him that, number one, he was never going to be able to get Southern Illinois University to take over. That's not the proper word, to acquire Sangamon State

University. I think the lieutenant governor, along with a variety of other people, including officials from the University of Illinois, told Senator Dunn, "We don't have any interest in ever making that medical school part of the University of Illinois." Ralph, I think, acquiesced to them. It's my guess the governor's office also talked to Senator Dunn, although I think most of the heavy pressure on Senator Dunn in terms of convincing him was done by the lieutenant governor himself.

Phil Adams, liaison for the regency system, agreed: "I know why he voted for this bill. He voted for this bill after he looked Garrett Deakin [liaison for SIU] and me in the eye and said he wouldn't. Because Bob Kustra told him, 'I will guarantee that SIU is on the Board of Higher Ed,' and that's what it's all about. That's like giving away sweat in August, man. That is nothing." Alluding to bad fortunes in SIU leadership—an acting chancellor, a Carbondale president recovering from a heart attack—Adams says, "They had an opportunity, probably not to get Sangamon, but certainly to get themselves taken care of. . . . They didn't get much out of it."

Senator Vince Demuzio was strongly in favor of the restructure concept, had favored it in 1993, and would have worked for it in 1995. He wanted SSU in the U of I system, but not at the expense of the SSU union:

> In my view, I don't think the governor cared. I don't think Bob Kustra cared. I think it was a provision that Ikenberry put in. . . . I think the labor provision was one provision that he absolutely had to have. I think he was trying to satisfy the academic community, basically at Champaign, because they have not been in favor of teachers' unions in the university. . . . The [Republican leadership] rounded up the votes that were necessary to pass it with that provision in there. But I give Stanley Ikenberry, in my judgment, total credit for that provision being added. I don't think it came from the [Edgar] administration in any way, shape, or form.

The bill passed the senate with 33 votes, with 30 votes the minimum required. I teased Demuzio, asking what he would have done had the call stuck on 29? He replied, "It would have been a tough vote. . . . I doubt that I would have been the 30th vote with that provision still in there."

Barbara Currie, Democratic leader in the House, assessed the consequences for the teachers' union but did not perceive much punch from the AFL/CIO:

> Well, I feel sorry for the union, but on the other hand, it was in the cards. If it's going to happen, it's going to happen. And U of I is not going to unionize any time soon. I believe there is a very active AAUP at the U of I. So that will be an alternate way for faculty grievances and faculty issues to be addressed, but certainly the collective bargaining—that is, the way you've done business

at Sangamon State—is unlikely to persist in the future. There was not a large hue and cry on that topic. And while, of course, the UPI—

*Van Der Slik:* There was some showing of the flag.

*Currie:* UPI Professionals did their number, but you didn't see this as a major issue with AFL-CIO. And I suppose the answer is that it's a very localized phenomenon, a local thunderstorm. There's always the possibility that Sangamon State's way of doing business will expand to the University of Illinois, although I think that's extremely unlikely.

The result was passage of the primary legislation to restructure the system of systems. The only substantive accommodation that the political leaders made was to change SSU's bargaining unit. It gave Democrats talking points against the bill, but as long as the administration and Republican legislative leaders were together on the matter, the policy was destined for easy passage.

### *Muzzling the Other Education Policy Leaders*

In 1993, there was some visibility of the educational policy leaders, particularly the system heads at the BOR and BOG, in offering criticism about the original restructuring proposal. As noted before, they did not elaborate on or advocate different alternatives. Their position was that the system of systems was better than other alternatives. They were part of a larger consensus to preserve the status quo. Dissident campus presidents were a small minority and were not conspicuous in the legislative process. As already noted, NIU's La Tourette had a pat public response, paraphrased as, "I will live with the legislative reality."

Following the first-round legislative defeat in 1993, the governor and lieutenant governor moved toward their preferred policy with leverage in their hands. Boards for three systems other than the U of I were appointive. The administration could defuse opposition by means of strategic board appointments. According to Kustra:

> I won't go so far as to say that we appoint board members who we then give specific instructions regarding what their chancellor should or shouldn't do. I would say that two years ago, when we failed the first time, thanks to Madigan's majority, I can remember the governor saying, "What we cannot accomplish through this reorganization legislation, we will at least accomplish in part through the appointment process." And he was focused singularly on finding people who would agree with us that the ultimate solution to the organization of higher education in Illinois must be that each of these universities would have their own boards. So unless they lied to us, no one was going to get on a board that wasn't in support of our agenda. At that time, you know, we didn't know for sure when we would resurface this agenda.

Later, he added, "We certainly were aware that we needed to find people for the system boards who were in support of our agenda."

By 1995, this had the effect of limiting the opposition that might have come from the chancellors of the two most affected boards. Layzell responded to my question about lobbying in 1993:

> I was directly involved as probably you remember. In fact, Kustra complained openly a few times about my involvement with editorial boards and legislators and legislative committees. Bob and I kind of jousted with each other over 3 or 4 months, and, of course, the discussion of this was great. And the presidents were involved also, some more than others in terms of their discussions of the issue. Because this issue affected the board, I thought it was an important public policy debate. In fact, at that time, the board directed me to register opposition to the proposal and to provide information to legislators and others about it. So I got personally involved.

However, in 1995, Layzell's position was much more circumspect: "I recommended [at the January 19, 1995, board meeting] that at that point that they take a neutral position. The board had changed since 1993. We had lost some members who had been there in 1993 so that the level of understanding and feeling about it was different than it was two years ago." So Layzell did not advocate pro or con on the issue. Groves was more specific. He observed:

> As Bob Kustra said, members of the boards have been appointed by this Governor. At the minimum, the Governor makes it very well known to the appointees of our boards what the administration position is on governance. At the maximum, it says that they want a commitment.
>
> *Van Der Slik:* So there was a litmus test? Is that too strong a word?
>
> *Groves:* I think that is too strong a word, but I think that what has been made very clear, judging from Bob Kustra's comments, is that in fact people were appointed to these boards after they had been queried about their position on reorganization, after they had been talked to with regards to the administration's position on reorganization, after the administration was convinced that they would not be strong opponents of reorganization. And so that puts me—both me and Tom Layzell—on very shaky ground in terms of doing any representation. I made it my point to say I was speaking for myself and not the board. The reason for that is, frankly, it hadn't been discussed before, and I don't know what way the board would go on it. Another thing is, I must say that we haven't discussed it with the board because it hasn't come up. Our last meeting was in January, and at that time, the Governor had made his speech, and we had a general idea, but we did not have legislation, and we did not discuss it with our Board because we didn't think it was going to be passed.

And, he added, compared to previously, "I have sensed [in board members] a much greater awareness of interest and concern about what is going on politically as the whole reorganization campaign heated up." So the Edgar administration moved aggressively on board appointments. Ross Hodel, deputy director of the IBHE, noted that Edgar's board appointments were much more prompt than had been the case previously under Governor James Thompson, indicating that these appointments were of greater importance to Edgar.

Finally, it is noteworthy that the executive director of the IBHE, Richard Wagner, had no say in shaping the restructuring. The governor's task force report was made to the governor, not the IBHE. As noted previously, the IBHE's own most recent report, from the Committee on Scope, Structure, and Productivity, was issued in 1990 and called for no structural changes. So when the issue was before the legislature in 1993, Wagner said: "I wasn't involved in making the proposals. They came from a different source." Asked if Kustra and Edgar sought advice about particular choices to be made, Wagner answered: "No. Others made those decisions." Wagner's board chair, Art Quern, was obviously associated with the governor's proposals, having cochaired the task force. It is fair to say that the education policy professionals were silenced by the administration, and the means for doing so was available and exercised in the governor's appointments of new members to the boards of the systems and the IBHE.

*Republican Tactics: Fast Track*

"Fast track" borrows a term from the federal trade policy-making process. Congress has approved a procedural arrangement so that the president can negotiate a trade agreement with foreign countries and submit it to them. Once submitted, Congress cannot amend it and must vote it up or down within ninety days. Presidents have found that other nations are reluctant to agree to a deal if subsequently the Congress can force a second round of negotiations (for more discussion, see Rubin 1997, 162). Action in ninety days without amendments is a major procedural concession for Congress to make.

In 1995, the new Republican majority in the Illinois House and a supplemented majority in the Senate did not formalize the concept of a fast track. But as a matter of strategy, Senate President Pate Philip, Speaker Lee Daniels, and Governor Jim Edgar did agree to make all due speed in adopting a series of major policy changes. Mike Lawrence, the governor's press secretary, explained:

> Well, you know, two days after the governor was reelected, it was two or three days after, he met with Philip and Daniels. He told them he thought it would be a good idea for them to define certain areas that they could agree on and to move quickly on those areas.

*Van Der Slik:* When the governor was elected, you're really talking about the second time?

*Lawrence:* Yes.

*Van Der Slik:* And Republicans had the majority in both houses?

*Lawrence:* Exactly. He met with the leaders. He basically said, "Look, we now have majorities in both legislative chambers and the governor's office. We need to demonstrate that we're going to exercise leadership. There were certain things that had been held up because of gridlock, and we need to demonstrate now that we can move ahead." The Scaffolding Act, tort reform, welfare reform, some anticrime measures—those were on the table, and the governor put the higher education reorganization on the table. It had been held up in, I think, at least two previous sessions of the legislature. So he himself put it on the table.

Speaker Daniels later reported to his district constituents that "we formulated a 'Fast Track' agenda to address issues including crime, taxes, education, health care and the economy" (Daniels 1995b). The Speaker's summary of fast-track legislation listed fifteen items. In practice, the idea was to adopt legislation with cohesive Republican majorities, avoiding much bipartisan horse trading. The agenda emphasized a probusiness slant. Representative David Wirsing explained the approach while describing why the opponents were resigned to losing on this issue: "First of all, they knew what fast track was. They knew that each of those fast track items were a very precise piece of legislation that minimally all the Republicans including the governor could sign on to, that they could vote for in committee, and in chambers, house and senate both. That's basically what those fast track pieces were. Some reform in a different direction. So this was part of the education package, and I think they all realized this thing was going to happen. It was going to go." The decision regarding what would be included on the fast track was made by the governor and two legislative leaders. This one, according to Kustra, was the governor's choice. It was he who said, "Put higher ed on." For Tom Ryder, Republican deputy majority leader, this restructure was something that fit the Republican philosophy:

> First of all, it was not a new idea. The lieutenant governor and the individuals that I mentioned had been out promoting the idea for quite some time. It fit with a Republican tendency of reducing bureaucracy. As a symbol, the change was being made by the Republicans that were in town. So it fit the fast-track criteria. It also fit because it was something that all sides could sign off on fairly quickly, which was a prerequisite for fast-track.

*Van Der Slik:* Both sides, meaning—

*Ryder:* House, Senate, and Executive.

*Van Der Slik:* In terms of the Republicans?

*Ryder:* Yes. Sure. The Republicans are the only ones that agreed to fast-track. . . . The speaker clearly adopted it early, as I recall. This was one of those items that was the quickest to come together. It was one that when leadership sat down and said, "What are fast-tracked items? What is it we're going to do?"— it was on the list from my earliest memory. I think that's because of the players—the Kustra, the Weaver, and the Dillard, and the governor—who had laid the groundwork. In leadership, it was always on the list. To my recollection, there was no objection.

Not surprisingly, the reasons that made fast track attractive to Republicans made it painful to Democrats. According to Representative Art Turner:

So this fast track is just saying, "Hey, look, we came here in January, and we got busy. We've changed seven or eight major pieces of legislation or legislative issues. We've dealt with tort reform. We've dealt with welfare reform. We've changed higher ed. We've dealt with school mandates. We put the issue out here, the scaffolding act." I think that that's just all part of this national Republican agenda to say, "Look, we're busy. We know what we want to do. We don't have to sit around and debate it." In fact, there was very little debate. The bill hit the floor, and they said, "Here it is." I think that given a chance to debate this issue that they might have gotten some additional input that I think probably was well worth discussing. They've got the votes. I think it was unfair the way this bill was presented. There was no opportunity to consider the idea of all schools being U of I or of U of I Chicago having a separate board. So that tells you that it was certainly orchestrated by one or two and no real legislative input. I think it was just part of the fast track for the Republicans to prove that they're much more efficient. Actually, they're proving that they're much more dictatorial, but I think that was just part of their overall agenda of saying, "Hey, we're getting it on. We're out of here by June 1." I think some of this, in fact I'm sure, is going to come back to haunt them.

For Art Quern, the IBHE chair, the fast track made sense because Republicans knew and were united about what they wanted to do. It was not substantively partisan, but tactically so. "You've got a Republican governor. They're identifying certain things that show that they are able to get things done. So they fast track certain things. The Democrats, naturally enough, don't want them to have those victories, so they try to stop those things. I don't think the substance is the focal point of the partisanship; it's the process that is the partisanship. . . . Once you have it on the fast track, it has an impact of an electrifying machine. You're either for it or against it." Democratic Senator Vince Demuzio, despite not being able to vote for the bill because of the union issue, supported the concept of the change. Commenting on the effectiveness of the fast track tactic, he noted: "I did agree with that. The opportunity for affiliation [of SSU] with the University of Illinois might never rise again. They were quite sure they had to move as quickly as they could. In talking to Kustra, I advised moving along as quickly as possible as well."

The fast track inhibited adjustments, amendments, variations, and the cooling of Republican élan to put through another major piece of legislation. As Democratic staffer Everson could see from the opposition side: "We had heard that there were at least a handful of their members that did not want to vote for this. But there was all the pressure of fast track. They were able to get 63 of their members to vote for tort reform. That is certainly more difficult than getting 64 of their members to vote for higher ed reorganization. There were just so many of their members that didn't really have a stake in this but who bought the argument that this is important. People in their party just went along with it." Ettinger likewise commented, under pressure from Kustra, that Republicans who had expressed reservations, simply caved in: "I think had this not been on the fast track, had this not been a top issue with more than a desperately needed show of strength and unanimity and discipline, we could have adjusted this thing. But, as somebody put it in a newsletter, we were road kill on the fast track."

## Alternatives from Interest Groups

Since the publication of *A Nation at Risk* (National Commission on Excellence in Education 1983), there have been surges of change and reform in elementary and secondary education in Illinois as well as nationwide. Numerous interest groups have been active, offering policy alternatives and battling for favored options while resisting the intrusions of others. Obvious perennial players include the Illinois Education Association, the Illinois Federation of Teachers, the Illinois Association of School Administrators, and the Illinois Association of School Boards. But there are a variety of specialized and regional organizations, such as the Large Unit District Association, Educational Research and Development, South Cook Public Education, and the Local Education Network of DuPage County. Groups have risen with acronyms such as LO-CON, for local control, and FAIRCOM, which tries to defend its high-tax-base districts. However, as the battles for schools have engaged issues such as property tax rates and caps and proposals to raise income tax on personal and corporate taxes, some of the major peak groups of Illinois—the Farm Bureau, the Illinois Chamber of Commerce, and the Illinois Manufacturers—have weighed in on education issues. These groups raise the attention of AFSCME and the AFL-CIO. Regional battles were fought by forces marshaled by the mayors of Chicago, suburban Republicans, and downstate interests. Elementary and secondary education has evoked a wide and enduring series of political battles that activate high group interest and participation (for a good introduction, see Gove and Nowlan 1996, 177–92).

Quite in contrast with lower-level education, higher education has been little affected by interest groups. Skirmishing has primarily reflected turf battles, tuition rates, and, among public institutions, getting their fair share of public funds. Unionization came to the BOG schools in 1975, to Sangamon State in 1986, and SIUC in 1997. But these groups have a narrow focus. When higher education restructuring came on to the decision agenda, no groups were activated by it. None perceived stakes in the issue. Richard Wagner, executive director of the IBHE, drew some comparisons to elementary and secondary education:

> First of all, I think higher education gets generally good marks from the public and the special interest groups in terms of performance and services provided. Sure, there are problems. Costs and accountability and things we're working on. But I think there's a fair amount of respect across the state for higher

education. I think the mind-set out there was, "Hey, it's working pretty well. What is this all about?" In fact, I think if you talk to the individual members of the General Assembly, a lot of them would say, "Hey, what's this all about? Why are we doing this?" There were three or four people who felt passionately about it.

*Van Der Slik:* And were in a position to leverage the change?

*Wagner:* Yes. And so we're changing.

*Van Der Slik:* What was reformed thirty years ago is now the object of another reform now.

*Wagner:* Yes. You can compare our situation to school reform initiatives for elementary and secondary. Unfortunately, they go through a reform initiative every two years. You're absolutely right. There's many people involved in that process. And I think part of it is, "Hey, they are not getting the job done." There's dissatisfaction. You don't have that general feeling about higher education I think. I'm not saying everything is hunky dory with higher education. But you don't have that general feeling. So a lot of people had a hard time understanding what this was all about. But again, I answered the first question on election night 1994. I knew this was going to happen.

*Van Der Slik:* I'll interpret what you're saying as one of the marks of success of the IBHE and the IBHE staff. You have kept higher education a relatively low visibility matter and not become engaged in the pulling and hauling by the groups.

*Wagner:* Well, I'd put it different way. I won't say the IBHE and the IBHE staff, Jack. I'd just say the system of higher education has been able to achieve a fairly high level performance and accountability that has merited the general support of the public. I think the IBHE has a role to play in that. But others certainly had a major role. Faculty and the delivery of instruction is what it is all about in many respects. So I would say the higher education system collectively has been able to do that.

Rod Groves of the Regency System agreed:

> I think that there is perception out there that higher education ain't broke. I mean higher education is doing just fine. They don't get any feedback from opposition. The most that they get is from students from time to time who say, "Why are tuition bills going up?" But you don't get a whole lot of consternation on that score. So by and large I think there is this perception that higher education is in pretty good shape. It's taking care of itself pretty well. The Governor wants to or the Lt. Governor want to move the pieces around. Well, I guess that's okay. No big deal. Surely nothing to oppose. Probably not anything to support either. If they want our support, they can call us.

Tom Layzell, chancellor of the BOG, was as vulnerable in the change as Groves. He was the only one to comment on the role of private colleges and the Federation of Independent Illinois Colleges and Universities, whose director was Donald Fouts. Layzell noted some interests and opposition to the proposed restructure in 1993, but by 1995, that interest had dissolved:

> Fouts and I was thinking more of people like Rich Stevens and Don Monday. Rich Stevens is President of the Danville College, and Don is Illinois College, and Father Richardson of DePaul. They were people that thought it was a bad idea and said so. Don, I don't remember what Don's involvement was. I don't remember Don Fouts being out—strongly supportive of the changes, and so he was neutral at best. But there were people in the federation and presidents in the federation who were concerned about the breakup of the system. I assume they probably were this year, but you just didn't hear much out of them.

It can be noted that the recent comparative study of state governance structures (Bowen et al. 1997, 40) made the observation that the form of higher education governance in Illinois has dampened adversarial relationships between the public and private sectors. In this particular matter, the private sector spokespersons maintained disinterested silence in this public sector policy action.

In the legislative process, except for the union issue regarding SSU, groups were silent. Democratic Representative Currie noted that interest groups just were not interested in this matter. Democrat Art Turner explained it with partisanship and the fast track:

> It's been the Republican's way of how they're handling all these issues. They're not allowing interest groups, no one, any real input into the major decisions here in the state. I think it's going to come back to haunt them for that very reason. They've pretty much shut off all debate. They say, "While the Democrats were in control the last twelve, you had time to debate. We've heard the debate, and it has not been rectified. We have the answers." And so this is the approach that they're taking with most of the issues. They're changing rules here in the house and in the senate over the last couple of years. It's kind of a democracy that one hates to read about, but it's one that really scares you. From one who is wearing the hat of the double minority, it's very scary.

But Republican Mike Weaver said higher education is not relevant to the peak groups who enter the conflict about elementary and secondary education:

> To a lot of groups like that, and I don't want to point to anyone specifically, but higher education is kind of a black hole. An unknown for them. They really don't know where to place—a lot of folks in those areas think of higher education as a luxury. They have to deal mainly with the results of our elementary and secondary system 90 percent of the time and only when they start looking for mid or higher level management people do they even bother with higher education. So I think they pretty much stayed away from it because they don't know what it does or what it's supposed to do for them.

This was not an issue that affected other groups. Generally speaking, few groups concern themselves about higher education. The education unions have bread-and-butter interests, and the decommissioning of SSU's union did get some AFL-CIO response. But it was hardly a central concern. For others, the governor's desire to move the furniture in higher education did not evoke response even from the private universities, and the public universities had themselves been silenced. Other politically active major groups, such as the medical society, manufacturers, realtors, chambers of commerce, agribusiness interests, and the like, tended to their own affairs, looking on this issue merely as spectators.

## Constituency Interests

Constituency interests did not activate the development of policy alternatives. There was, however, one type of active constituency. That was the university towns. One in particular was significant during the policy development stage. The Springfield local community, through some of its community leaders, did press for inclusion of Sangamon State into the University of Illinois system. Democratic Senator Vince Demuzio, whose district is just southwest of Springfield, and who has a master's degree from Sangamon State, was involved early with the Springfield Chamber of Commerce:

> As a matter of fact, they were supporting Sangamon State and the U of I without taking the position on the governor's reform. They were for Springfield becoming a free standing branch of the university. They were for reviewing the senior institution status by the new governing board, with input from the community with regard to the existing higher education programs within the community. So, there was some concern as to what focus Sangamon may or may not have now or in the future. I think all the major players in Springfield were on board from the beginning. There were some apprehensions about four year institutions and what might happen in the future to the community college and maybe the Springfield College and the private higher ed stuff. But, I think, generally speaking, most people felt that would be a good thing not only for the community but for good policy innovation and creativity. Perhaps it is good for both Sangamon State University as well University of Illinois and perhaps the state. And in the process, we enhance educational opportunities for those working in and with our state government and local government. Well, I agree.

Samuel Gove, the emeritus director of the U of I's Institute for Government and Public Affairs, noted the importance of Tom Lamont in the Springfield community. Active as an attorney and lobbyist, he was elected to the U of I board and served as its chair. "Tom Lamont, coming from Springfield, a very strong man, helped crank up the Springfield Chamber of Commerce and all those people. Bill Hanley was getting in touch with them. In fact, I've got a letter from Naomi

Lynn [president of Sangamon State University]. Someplace, there was a list of people who were on the promotion committee, I guess you would call it, to make Sangamon State part of the U of I." When interviewed, however, Lamont acknowledged his proponent's role in advocating for the inclusion of SSU during the consideration process but downplayed his role in the local community. But Lamont gave the community interest a direct voice on the U of I board.

Ikenberry acknowledged the importance of that connection when the question at stake was the acceptability of SSU:

> I think our board had very mixed views. I think we had trustees, for example, who came from the Springfield area—I think they were very enthusiastic about the prospect of U of I and Sangamon State joined together. I think there were other trustees who were more concerned about that union working well over the long term. Would it change the focus of attention at the university? I don't think there were extreme views, however, or strongly held extreme views on either end. Generally, interest ranged all the way from relatively strong to significant caution. But no strong opposition or do-or-die advocacy.

Rod Groves, the regency system chancellor, was also aware of the Springfield constituency and that SSU President Lynn's "role" was an active one: "I think her role has not been incorrect in this. I don't mean to be critical when I say that. I think President Lynn has weighed the situation with this community. I think that a good deal of the community support for this stemmed from sources that were close to the president and had her encouragement." Republican Senator Kirk Dillard thought the Springfield community's preference for the U of I affiliation rather than SIU helped confirm that choice, so he credited "the business leaders and civic leaders [of Springfield who] wanted Sangamon State to be part of the University of Illinois."

Ettinger, the union proponent for whom the bargaining unit issue was the overriding one, cheerlessly acknowledged the importance of the local advocacy and the Springfield Chamber of Commerce, along with President Lynn's advisory group:

> So Mike Boer [Springfield Chamber of Commerce] was part of her group, and they've been working towards this merger for quite sometime. I don't think that they were involved in any kind of conspiracy on the union front. But I know that they've been heavily involved in wanting to bring a four-year school to Springfield, and just looking at that list of names on her group, they're pretty gung-ho U of I types. Former trustees, alumni—it was pretty much a stacked deck on that front. Most of us didn't really mind; that was not a great concern. But when Mike Boer, representing Chamber, and Bill Hanley, representing Chamber, and Bill Forsyth, representing the president's group, all filed in favor of the bill, and knowing full well that it contained this anti-union component, I was upset with them and with the president, for not being straight

with us. I really am. After that session, Bob Sipe [union local president] and I went out to lunch with Bill Forsyth, and it was obvious to us that these folks were just so anxious to get the U of I here in their own backyard that it wouldn't matter. They would sell out their own mothers, it seemed to us.

In general, however, the restructure bill was not spoken of as a bill with constituency interest, a fact that was acknowledged by two opposing House Democrats, Currie and Turner. Currie resides in the Hyde Park area of Chicago. Her spouse is a law professor at the University of Chicago, and she is accessible to people of the Chicago universities. According to Currie: "On every campus, there were people who were for it and people who were against it. And I would be very surprised if in most places there was much passion. Did faculty members at Northeastern, Chicago State University, and Governors State, as well as UIC, have opinions? If they did, none of those individuals, neither students nor faculty from my district, said anything to me. Nary a word, nary a peep." Art Turner did not consider it very crucial to people in higher education: "I think for the average citizen on the street, this doesn't ring a bell to him, doesn't mean anything. He's more concerned about how he's going to pay his kid's tuition versus who's running the institution. It just wasn't a high profile issue, the importance of which I don't think the average citizen would care."

## Conclusion

Despite a usually open and pluralistically populated political system, little in the way of policy alternatives to the restructure proposal from the Edgar administration emerged throughout the policy process. In 1993, opponents did not change it—they defeated it. In 1995, it came back with one substantive change, which came from the policy community—specifically the U of I administration—and was promptly passed without further alterations.

The adoption was facilitated by the fact that the issue of SSU's union was resolved to the University of Illinois' satisfaction. At Ikenberry's request, the Edgar administration simply merged SSU into the larger single bargaining unit of the U of I.

The Edgar administration headed off alternatives by putting this bill onto a fast track. In short, it meant that Republican leaders agreed with the administration on what would work to pass with Republican votes. Democrats could concur, of course. But if they opposed, there were Republican majorities to pass the legislation anyway. The restructure went through as proposed without amendments.

Policy specialists in public universities with stakes in the changes were largely muzzled. In 1993, the BOR and BOG system heads were openly in opposition, although killing the bill was largely viewed as a partisan accomplishment by House Democrats. By 1995, Governor Edgar had used his power of appointment to change several board members on the BOR, BOG, and IBHE. By 1995, the chancellors had been neutralized. Several campus presidents were known to want independence. So alternatives were not specified. Republicans had the votes to pass the necessary legislation.

Interest groups were not interested in higher education governance. Labor had been neutralized by the fast track and the fact that SSU just was not important enough for labor to make a full court press. No other groups were activated by this issue. There were no general tax and spending implications.

Constituents did not stimulate the interests of individual legislators in this issue. The only conspicuously active constituency was that in Springfield, and the policy arena it most affected was the University of Illinois central administration and board. Springfield representatives could and did comfortably support the governor's proposal over the objections of an outflanked campus union at SSU. Opponents of the legislation did not resist the legislation because of constituent pressure. In fact, general constituent interest was nil.

In short, the Republican administration got its way by preempting policy alternatives.

# 5 | Electoral Results and Policy Change

A nalyses of national policy-making emphasize the role of the president. Presidents have some extraordinary tools for providing policy direction, not least of which is their status in the world, including their ability as commander-in-chief to exercise the superpower resources of this nation. But even in the domestic domain, their wishes receive impetus when they can meet popular expectations. Presidents can obtain a national forum on a moment's notice, and their policy appeals receive habitual attention. But, as Charles O. Jones (1995) notes about the presidential roles in the policy process, "it is apparent that the president's agenda-setting function varies considerably over time and across issues" (78). Jones goes on to offer a framework of analysis for that variation over recent presidents.

In state policy-making, governors have a substantial array of executive tools for leading the policy-making process. Governors cannot use the world stage to accomplish domestic policy purposes, but some of their institutional resources in the state policy environment are more powerful than those of the president. In Illinois, for example, the veto powers of the governor are much more elaborate than those of the president and add notably to the governor's ability to control budgetary alternatives and end runs by both legislators and bureaucrats. Although the parallels between presidents and governors may not be precisely alike, they are close enough to look for explanatory power in Jones's framework.

Jones focused on six presidents, but especially the five transitions between presidents. For each transition, he looked at the *agency orientation,* the broad trends in government just before the new president stepped into office. To simplify description, he labeled the context as expansive (growing), consolidative (integrating existing policies), contractive (reducing), and fiscal (stringency). *Agenda alternatives* refers to the degree to which presidents dominate the agenda, controlling the alternatives. The extent to which major policymakers are in substantial agreement about what is to be done in and by public policy is referred to as *agenda congruity.* Low congruity means the chief executive "is forced to compete with many other sources of policy alternatives" (80). What Jones found was that only two recent presidents controlled the agenda alternatives and achieved high agenda congruity. Those were Lyndon Johnson and Ronald Reagan. The others, Nixon, Ford, and Carter, were not able to control agenda alternatives and had much competition that resulted in policy alternatives they did not want.

While Jones's analysis is helpful, he limited his analysis to transitions. He pays little attention to second terms and, of course, only two presidents gained reelection during the period of his inquiry. Nixon's was short lived, and Reagan's was not noteworthy for policy success as was his first.

The domestic policy under scrutiny here is the restructuring of higher education. It was proposed in the middle of the Edgar-Kustra first term and won adoption on its second time around in the first year of the Edgar-Kustra second term. I propose to see what Jones's categories of analysis reveal about the disposition of the higher education restructure. For present purposes, however, I will look at three transitions. The first is the one occurring when Edgar-Kustra first took office. The second is following the mid-term election of 1992. The third follows the reelection year of 1994. As has already been shown, there was not a competition of policy ideas and alternatives during the process of restructuring higher education. Victories and defeats were had in the political stream.

## The Succession of Agendas

The variations that faced the Edgar-Kustra administration were in shifting political circumstances that altered both what might be achieved and what actually was accomplished.

### 1990

In 1990, there was no partisan turnover at the gubernatorial election. Republican James R. Thompson, four times elected in the previous fourteen years, stepped down voluntarily. Edgar and Kustra defeated Democrats Neil Hartigan and Jim Burns with 50.7 percent of the vote, compared to 48.2 percent for their rivals. Another 1.1 percent went to third-party candidates. It was hardly a mandate election. The well-matched gubernatorial candidates both had previously held statewide elective office. Edgar served ten years and was twice elected secretary of state. Hartigan had been twice elected attorney general and previously lieutenant governor for a term with Democrat Dan Walker (1973–77). At the same election, Republicans held on to the secretary of state position while Democrats retained attorney general, comptroller, and treasurer offices. Democrats upped their membership in the House by five members, from 67 to 72, and retained a 31 to 28 edge in the Senate.

As the table indicates, in 1990 there was stability in the legislative membership. In both chambers and in both parties, member continuity was high. In the Senate, there was no change at all—incumbents on both sides seeking and winning retention. The legislative leaders all stayed in place. There was not much fresh air let into either legislative party by the election.

**Incumbent Return**

| 1990 | House | | | | Senate[*] | | | |
|---|---|---|---|---|---|---|---|---|
| | Democrats | | Republicans | | Democrats | | Republicans | |
| | % | No. | % | No. | % | No. | % | No. |
| Preelection party balance | | 66 | | 52 | | 31 | | 28 |
| Seeking reelection | 94 | 65 | 94 | 46 | 100 | 10 | 100 | 10 |
| Relected | 98 | 61 | 88 | 43 | 100 | 10 | 100 | 10 |
| Returning | 92 | 61 | 82 | 43 | 100 | 10 | 100 | 10 |
| Postelection party balance | | 72 | | 46 | | 31 | | 28 |

[*]There were twenty Senate contests in 1990.

| 1992 | House | | | | Senate[*] | | | |
|---|---|---|---|---|---|---|---|---|
| | Democrats | | Republicans | | Democrats | | Republicans | |
| | % | No. | % | No. | % | No. | % | No. |
| Preelection party balance | | 72 | | 46 | | 31 | | 28 |
| Seeking reelection | 82 | 59 | 74 | 34 | 74 | 23 | 71 | 20 |
| Relected | 80 | 47 | 71 | 24 | 78 | 18 | 95 | 19 |
| Returning | 65 | 47 | 52 | 24 | 58 | 18 | 68 | 19 |
| Postelection party balance | | 67 | | 51 | | 27 | | 32 |

[*]There were fifty-nine Senate contests in 1992.

| 1994 | House | | | | Senate[*] | | | |
|---|---|---|---|---|---|---|---|---|
| | Democrats | | Republicans | | Democrats | | Republicans | |
| | % | No. | % | No. | % | No. | % | No. |
| Preelection party balance | | 67 | | 51 | | 27 | | 32 |
| Seeking reelection | 88 | 59 | 96 | 51 | 91 | 10 | 100 | 10 |
| Relected | 76 | 45 | 100 | 49 | 90 | 9 | 100 | 10 |
| Returning | 67 | 45 | 96 | 49 | 82 | 9 | 100 | 10 |
| Postelection party balance | | 54 | | 64 | | 26 | | 33 |

[*]There were twenty-one Senate contests in 1994.

By the time Jim Edgar got into office, it was clear that the nation was going into an economic decline and that revenue forecasts for state government were pretty pessimistic. According to Charles N. Wheeler (1991a), writing for the January *Illinois Issues,* belt tightening was to be the order of the day, with cuts coming in the budget that Edgar would promptly have to propose. Those cuts would be even more drastic if a temporary income tax rate hike already in place were not renewed. Democrat Hartigan opposed the income tax rate extension, but Edgar had campaigned with the argument that the increased rate should be made permanent. However, to do so was expected to require bipartisan support in the Democratic controlled legislature. Only nine of seventy-nine Republican legislators had supported the temporary increase in 1989. The agenda orientation for the new administration clearly needed to be contractive, because accompanying Edgar's support for the income tax increase, he made a strong "no new taxes" pledge.

It is not necessary to review Edgar's first legislative session here, but Wheeler (1991b) provided a capsule: "In truth, the rookie chief executive did very well in his first legislative session [as governor]. He delivered on major campaign promises to balance the budget without higher taxes—keeping the 20 percent income tax surcharge in place—and to cap skyrocketing real estate taxes" (10) The higher education restructuring idea had been proposed, as Kustra described, on an early 1991 outing in Macomb, Illinois, and discussed between himself and the governor. They agreed to form a task force.

In the higher education community, pressure for policy change was at the IBHE level, with initiative coming from Edgar's newly appointed board chair, Arthur Quern. Because he had been on Edgar's transition team looking specifically at budget and state finances, he knew as early as anyone in the Edgar administration how severe the early budget problems would be. Accepting the IBHE chairpersonship, he walked into early budget requests from the university systems "talking about 12, 15, 18 percent increases." Quern considered that his challenge:

> So I began to probe that. And when I started to get into the dialogue, they talked about how they had to do this, that, and the other thing. But nobody was talking about preserving the basic quality. And nobody was focusing on the basic round number of $2 billion that was being spent on public higher education. They were all talking about $30, $50, $80, $100 million incremental increase. And I realized that the parallels between what I was hearing there and what I was seeing throughout industry, and with all my clients, and in my own company, were dramatically clear. People tend to mouth words about quality, but not really to focus on what it takes to maintain quality. And that's where I got into the dynamic that you have to set some priorities; you have to pick that which is most important.

Quern gave great energy to the scrutiny of the systems and institutions through the PQP (Priorities, Quality, and Productivity) study mechanism. This initiative, later described as a "national model" by a California study team (Bowen et al. 1997), successfully aimed at increasing productivity in higher education. At the campus level, however, educators complained that Quern was transforming a deliberate and effective bottoms-up process into a top-down command model. Procedural and deadline pressures coming from the IBHE staff made a mess of the usual academic schedules and processes, to the great exasperation of the faculty and administrators who were supposed to make it work. Because some of the schools and systems did not act with alacrity, Quern went along with action to restructure governance. He made the connection this way: "So that is where I think the PQP and reorganization touched one another. It was the initial lack of response from the governing boards on this question of setting priorities and bringing people together to make some hard choices." Quern's concerns for PQP and perceptions of poor accountability within some campuses and system operations made him willing to cochair the task force that outlined the restructuring along with an appointed board for the U of I and a strengthening of coordinating powers for the IBHE. The task force was promised by Governor Edgar in his second budget message in March 1992. It gave a preliminary report in June and a final report in January 1993.

### 1992

While higher education was not a matter of visible interest in the partisan politics of 1992, it was a year of major change in partisan fortunes. Despite a substantial Clinton victory in the state, Republicans improved their numbers in the legislature. Republicans got a politically advantageous redistricting in 1991. Legislative leaders invested a new high in campaign spending, $11.5 million (Redfield 1995, 41). The result was a switch in partisan control in the Senate for Republicans for the first time in eighteen years. They obtained a 32 to 27 margin of control, losing only one incumbent, downing two Democratic incumbents, and gaining four seats. Senate leadership changed, of course. James "Pate" Philip, longtime Republican minority leader, became Senate president. Philip Rock, former Democratic leader, did not seek reelection, so after some intramural partisan scrapping, Chicagoan Emil Jones became the Democratic minority leader.

After a time of substantial membership stability, the new Senate had nine brand-new faces, thirteen senators up from the House, and three who had been appointed to Senate vacancies before the 1992 election (Pollock 1993). As the table shows, Republican incumbents fared much better than Democrats, of whom eight retired, including their leader, and five were defeated. For Republicans, eight retired, but only one was defeated.

Republicans could not overcome the Democratic advantage in the House but picked up five seats, making the Democratic advantage there 67 to 51. The house welcomed 47 new members out of 118, a major reshuffle in membership. Top leadership remained unchanged. Speaker Michael Madigan, Democrat leader since 1981, remained in charge, and Lee Daniels continued as minority leader, his post since 1983. About two-thirds of Democratic incumbents returned, but with so many House Republicans having moved on to the Senate, just over half of the Republicans elected were incumbents.

Commentators (Wheeler 1993a; Halperin 1993) on the governor's agenda in 1993 noted about as many items that he opposed as items that he was pushing. He would block increases in state income or sales taxes while making the previous income tax surcharge permanent. He would look for ways to get more services through administrative discipline. He would push for caps on local property tax increases (5 percent or the rate of inflation, whichever is less), tort reform with a cap on medical malpractice damage awards, heavier drug and crime penalties, alternative credentials for teachers, and reduced rules to allow nontraditional learning in some Chicago schools. In the mix would be restructuring higher education and changing governance. Budget growth was to be minimal. Although there was some optimism for economic recovery in the year ahead, an accumulation of Medicaid and welfare obligations cast a dark shadow over any likely budgetary flexibility. The agenda was in narrow fiscal straits, with the governor trying to reduce the state's obligations. The broad outlook for state government remained contractive.

With a Republican majority in the Senate and a more partisanly balanced, if still Democratically dominated, House, the governor's prospects for policy change were better than in the first two years. The partisan split gave the governor more bargaining leverage on interests he shared with Senate president Philip. However, with Democrats opposed to the higher education restructure, there was not a sense of agenda congruity. The session would be one of hard bargaining. The restructure proposal moved easily through the Senate but did not even get out of the higher education committee in the House. Opponents attacked not only the bill but also the motives of the governor (getting even for EIU president Rives's firing) and those of policy entrepreneur Kustra (doing something to improve his future electability). However, as noted previously, there was not activity to develop and promote alternatives, or change the mix of universities that would get their own boards. The administration's proposal was simply shot down politically. In the remainder of the biennium, the administration worked over its board appointees and set the issue of restructuring aside. According to Kustra: "At that time, you know, we didn't know for sure when we would resurface this agenda. I don't know what we would have done if the Republicans hadn't taken control of the Illinois house. I would probably have gone back and suggested we try it [again], but I've never asked the governor what his eventual decision would have been. He may have decided like we did last year [1994], 'Let's not kill ourselves.' I mean last year was an election year, so we knew that it wouldn't get very far. . . . We decided early on not to tackle it." The larger result of that session was a compromise settlement of the budget—one so thoroughly negotiated between Republicans and Democrats that there were no item vetoes and no reduction vetoes. The governor got a two-year Medicaid assessment plan approved, which gave breathing room for a growing economy to get the state's revenue picture into better shape (Wheeler 1993b).

## *1994*

A new political era began with the 1994 election in Illinois. Two of twenty congressional seats turned from Democratic to Republican, helping Newt Gingrich to a Republican majority in the U.S. House. In state politics, Republicans swept all the statewide executive offices. They carried everything but, ironically, one seat on the U of I Board of Trustees. For the first time since 1970, Republicans had majorities in both the House and Senate. In the Senate, they added one to their majority, now 33 to 26. Democrats lost only one incumbent in the Senate but got only three-quarters of their incumbents reelected. In the House, Republicans picked up thirteen seats, and all their incumbents were reelected, for a comfortable margin of 64 to 54. Jim Edgar and Bob Kustra won with a 64 to 34 margin with 2 percent scattered.

When the governor presented his state of the state speech in January, it disappointed commentators for its lack of imagination, but it was quite to the satisfaction of the new majorities. According to Wheeler (1995), "Edgar broke precious little new ground in his 36-minute address, offering instead a rehash of what has come to be the standard Republican agenda on some issues for the last two decades." Wheeler quoted Edgar, who laid out the early strategy for the session: "The presiding officers of this new, dramatically changed legislature and I agree. We need not wait until the closing hours of this legislative session to act responsibly and responsively on major reforms. . . . Property caps, tort reform to spur job creation, school reform, continued welfare-to-work initiatives and anti-crime legislation. I want all of it sent to me on a fast track."

What Wheeler's comment and the quotation from Edgar make clear is that there was an established Republican policy wish list. Items such as tort reform had been on it for a long time. Welfare-to-work was on both the national agenda and on that of most governors. Republican governors wanted to do the sort of things on welfare that Tommy Thompson was doing in Wisconsin and John Engler had going in Michigan. But in Illinois, Democratic leverage in the legislature had previously made that unattainable. After the 1994 election, Republicans promptly exercised their majorities in behalf of those unpassable ideas that had kicked around in bill form during earlier sessions. In Charles Jones's terms, there was a high degree of agenda congruity.

When the Republican leadership agreed on education reform, it referred to more than higher education restructuring. By session's end, the legislature would hand administrative control of Chicago schools to the city's Democratic mayor and adopt what critics would call a suburban-friendly state budget. But for Edgar and Kustra, university restructuring was suddenly an easy task. For the first time, Edgar could look expansively at the agenda and say which policies would have his mark. The governor and legislative leaders agreed to the main issues and agreed on the strategy of the fast track. There was, perhaps to a greater degree than in the Johnson and Reagan administrations that Jones examined, congruity about what solutions would be applied to which problems in Illinois.

## The Importance of Electoral Change

While it was up to Republicans to spell out the specifics of their policy congruity, those with stakes in the higher education restructure knew immediately that a sea of change had taken place. The consensus among my respondents was striking. My first question to Richard Wagner, IBHE executive director, was introduced by saying higher education organization has been subject to perennial scrutiny:

*Van Der Slik:* When did you realize this latest reorganization was going to pass?
*Wagner:* Election night, 1994.
*Van Der Slik:* You said to yourself, "Now it's going to happen."
*Wagner:* Yes.

Responses from others were similar if not as terse. Rod Groves noted that this policy issue was not very visible during the campaign:

> What I said was that if there was a Republican sweep, it would happen immediately after. I knew that was going to be the consequence because I knew the votes would be there by virtue of the fact that it wasn't an issue that was strongly articulated and grappled with in the campaign.

*Van Der Slik:* You are talking about the Governor's campaign in 1994?
*Groves:* Yes, in 1994. By virtue of the fact that it was not a highly visible component of last fall's campaign, it made it very likely that a Republican majority would have very few objections to the idea. I think it had a strong attraction and they'd have very few objections to it. I think the legislature just ratified it.

Lamont, the U of I board chair, perceived it similarly:

> I did not take it seriously again until this fall's election. Then I knew that this was to be a major agenda item of the Edgar administration. And, I thought, if that is the case, it is probably going to happen, particularly since the earlier proposal already passed out of the senate only to die in the house. If the house wasn't seen as an obstacle any longer, it was going to go. I understand that this was discussed within the first week subsequent to the election. The planning weeks, in November.

*Van Der Slik:* With the central administration?
*Lamont:* No. Discussed within the Edgar administration. In other words, the higher ed reorganization was a high priority to the Edgar administration, as I understand it. I was made aware of it, in passing. Of course, when the gover-

nor had his State of the State message, he again reentered it as what he wanted to see happen. I believed immediately that it was going to happen. Many of our fellow members had no real idea that it was happening. You had to read deep into the stories to see that this might happen. But we only had a limited amount of discussion at our board table, because it was not an agenda item to be discussed.

Adams, the designated defender of the regency system, saw the system's vulnerability in 1994 in partisan terms, "probably solely based on the November [1994] election. Clearly it would have never happened had Mike Madigan been able to hold the house." Ettinger, lobbyist for the University Professionals of Illinois, said: "My first premonition came the night of the elections, once we saw the sweep, that Edgar and Kustra would be ready to roll. And I think everybody who was close realized that would indeed be a priority. They'd been working on it for two or three years. The majority in both houses could easily deliver it." Paula Wolff saw the election outcome as "one precipitating event" and noted it as the point when restructure was a serious agenda item.

A clue to the governor's interest in the restructuring issue comes from Kirk Dillard. Now a senator, previously Edgar's chief of staff, he recalled that Edgar was anxious to trigger the change:

> On his inaugural night at the ball itself at the Prairie Capital Convention Center with all the things going on, Governor Edgar walked over to me. . . . He came over to me and—
>
> *Van Der Slik:* This is 1991?
>
> *Dillard:* This is 1995. He came over to me and said, "You're familiar with this issue. Like me, you have had an interest in it for twenty years"—because Jim sponsored a bill many years ago to do this. He said, "You work with the lieutenant governor, and you work with Art Quern on this a little bit in my office. I want you to sponsor the reorganization of higher ed act. You're a believer in it; you can explain it. If you're like me and around the capitol, you're also a history and nostalgia buff. I want you to sponsor this bill."

Thomas Layzell, BOG chancellor, could see the particularistic results of the legislative election. Not only had Edgar and Kustra won, but several of the House Democrats who had been publicly critical of the proposed restructure in 1993 had lost their seats in 1994: John Ostenburg, Terry Steczo, Mike Curran, and Bill Edley. Bob Kustra could not help but take some satisfaction in Edley's defeat. Edley, whose district included Macomb and Western Illinois University, had worked Kustra over pretty harshly in committee in the 1993 session.

*Kustra:* Another major opponent of the bill was Bill Edley, who we defeated in 1994.

*Van Der Slik:* And the Republican who came along was favorable?

*Kustra:* Rich Myers has been favorable all along. Rich Myers gave his maiden speech on the floor last week in favor of this bill, which is a really good example of real change through political turnover. I mean you have a guy who is against it; he gets defeated. A guy who wins comes aboard, and his first speech out of the box is in support of this particular piece of legislation.

Jones (1995) noted that presidents Johnson and Reagan succeeded to the presidency with strong endorsements for their agenda orientation, control over alternatives, and a strong degree of agenda congruity (99). However, he notes that even presidents who get their way early on face stiff competition later (99). The example here reveals changes biennium by biennium. If presidents rarely have better second terms than first, in Illinois Edgar and Kustra were rewarded for staying with their agenda and maintaining focus on their policy goals, after their second term gains in electoral success.

## Ambitious Decision-Making and Speculative Augmentation

In chapter 2, I took note of Jones's four-fold typology of policy decision-making based on two orthogonal dimensions (Jones 1977, 217–22). One is "estimated capacities." Jones refers to "the principal policy actors' estimates of knowledge." How deep is their degree of understanding of policy substance? Is it well communicated to those who participate in the decision-making? Is knowledge about administrative and political capabilities for putting change into effect part of that understanding? The other dimension, change, varies from incremental change to large change. Change includes, for example, law and policy, social behavior, physical conditions, and institutional change. What was the scope of change intended by the principle actors? Jones pinpointed as the most interesting quadrant of the four-fold table the one in which estimated capacities (understanding) is low but "an opportunity to act presents itself to those intending large change in policy." In 1995, Jones applied this framework to presidential decision-making. "Many of the achievements of the Johnson and Reagan administrations during the first few months fit into this fourth quadrant. Grand intentions were facilitated by an opportunity to act, even while acknowledging that the consequences of these actions were not known and that policy analytical capacities remained weak" (100).

How do these two dimensions—scope of change and estimated capacities—apply to the higher education restructuring? Let me address the extent of the change. In a sense, the change proposed was not huge. The system of systems was comprised of five elements: the University of Illinois, with two campuses; Southern Illinois University, with two campuses plus a Springfield medical school; the Board of Governors, with five universities, each bearing a distinct name; and the Board of Regents, with three distinctly named universities; and the Illinois Community College Board, overseeing forty-nine community colleges. Two of these elements, BOR and BOG, were broken up, with seven universities getting their own governing boards. Sangamon State was merged into the University of Illinois. The community college board ended up unchanged. The SIU system was untouched, although it was in play as the alternative system to absorb Sangamon State University.

On the other hand, the change was far from a matter of modest tinkering. The evolution of the system of systems took place between 1957 and the approval of the second higher education master plan in 1967. By then, the five systems were in place, although the two last state universities, Sangamon and Governors, came on-line in 1969. After that there were forays at change, which have already been described, particularly regarding Northern, ISU, and Eastern. It was a pet idea of Senator Sam Vadalabene, during the early 1980s, to get independence for SIUE. Representative Thomas McGann aired the idea for a separate existence of UIC. During his presidency, Stanley Ikenberry disavowed interest in making all the state universities into campuses of the University of Illinois. Singular changes never got anywhere. The system of systems prevailed, since the establishment of the IBHE in 1961 and the approval of the second master plan in 1967 (Matsler and Hines 1987, 17–35). To break up the system of systems in 1995 was not broadly conspicuous to Illinoisans, but in the scheme of governance for universities, it was a substantial policy change. In his comparative study of higher education restructuring, Marcus (1997) treats the Illinois revisions as a "major restructuring proposal" (409).

Besides the independent boards, another significant alteration was making the board of the University of Illinois appointive by the governor, rather than elective by the state at large. The election of trustees was established by a law enacted in 1887. So the 1995 change dismantled a century-old practice in favor of gubernatorial appointment with Senate confirmation. Edgar's proposed changes for higher education included a proposal to strengthen the powers of the IBHE to oversee the numerous independent universities. I shall examine that matter further below. It did not pass the legislature. After fast track, a legislative initiative to give community colleges greater programmatic latitude and take the Illinois Community College Board out from under IBHE coordination passed the legislature but was successfully vetoed by the governor. With restructuring once uncorked, some parties wanted even more change than did Edgar and Kustra. All in all, the scope of change attempted was very broad, and two of the three major initiatives wanted by the governor prevailed; an unwanted proposal rather late to the scene got legislative adoption but was put aside by the chief executive.

This policy change not only substantially altered a system in place for a generation, but the new system put in place will likely endure for some time. Republican Senator Kirk Dillard offered his assessment:

> I think we're doing it for twenty years. First of all, barring some major shift in public opinion, it's my guess that at least one chamber of the legislature will remain in Republican hands. But I don't think that a Democratic governor will come in and change it. Number one, there could be chaos, and you don't want

to make these changes every now and then. The governance system just leads to a lot of problems such as bond revenue for facilities. Changes just can't go back and forth. It is my guess that people on these campuses will like the new system much better than the old system. Even if Democrats control the legislature and the governor, it is my guess that people from Macomb, Charleston, Bloomington-Normal, and DeKalb won't want to change that system, and Springfield as well. I just think they won't change even if party control of government changes. I think the system that we've put in place with this new bill will work, and these communities won't let a Democratic governor and Democratic legislature change it. I think this system is here, if not forever, for twenty years.

Jones (1995) offers, as one of his conclusions from studying presidential transitions and agendas: "Control of policy alternatives and agenda congruity can contribute to ambitious decision making through speculative augmentation, which can in turn alter the agenda orientation for future presidents" (101).

By speculative, he means, as he said previously (1977), "a breakthrough is achieved despite the limits of knowledge" (221). The leaders proceed intuitively, not necessarily with a well-articulated rationale or theory about implications and consequences of the policy solution to be imposed. The policy change must be large—augmentative "if not actually quantum," according to Jones. I am concerned here to show that the estimated capability in this process was low. The change was pushed on faith, given an opportunity—indeed, an open window, in Kingdon's terms.

There were two key documents upon which the Edgar-Kustra restructuring was built. For simplicity, I will refer to them as Task Force Report One (TFR1) and Task Force Report Two (TFR2) (see Governor's Task Force on Higher Education 1992; Governor's Task Force on Higher Education 1993). TFR1 was presented to the governor on June 15, 1992. The report was five and one-half pages of single-spaced text, plus seven pages of appendix. It reviewed historical background, briefly described the existing system, lightly described past studies, and launched into recommendations for change. Leading into its recommendations, it quoted Aims McGuinness Jr., a national expert from the Education Commission of the States: "State interests are not necessarily the same as the sum of institutional interests." With that, the task force recommended the following:

> In an effort to better reflect the "state interests," this Task Force recommends that changes to the "system of systems" could improve the delivery and quality of services provided through our higher education system. Consideration must be given to cost efficiencies and program delivery. Although this issue has been thoroughly reviewed over time by this group and others, change should not be made hastily. If you, as Governor, decide to proceed with changes to the structure, we recommend a reconfiguration of institutions as suggested later in this report.

There upon the task force offered two optional forms of change. It then raised four issues "in the context of reorganization." First, the task force preferred Sangamon State to go to the U of I but allowed that SIU might be appropriate. Second, it would make U of I trustees appointive. Third, it would strengthen IBHE to "provide additional oversight and accountability" over the entire system. Fourth, it would change IBHE membership to reduce representation of specific systems on the board.

Six months later, TFR2, a four-page report, was presented. The rationale for its recommendation was in two paragraphs:

> The Task Force reviewed the work of past efforts to study the structure of higher education, invited written and oral testimony from interested individuals and discussed how to achieve increased cost effectiveness. We became convinced that history and tradition had left the structure of higher education with layers of oversight which have become cumbersome, which are too expensive to maintain, and most important, which blur the lines of accountability necessary to achieve increased productivity and cost effectiveness. As a result, we are recommending a simplified approach to govern public universities in Illinois—one that minimizes bureaucracy and clarifies the lines of authority.
>
> Just as the private sector and the rest of state government have faced the challenge of downsizing and reorganizing in the interest of cutting costs and increasing effectiveness, so too must higher education reduce middle management levels which have grown in power, salaries and staff, but which can no longer be justified in this new era of accountability and productivity.

The report offered seven recommendations. The first and most detailed was the restructure, dissolving two system boards, establishing individual governing boards for seven schools, and putting SSU into the U of I system. Points two and three dealt with appointive boards for the seven schools and that each board "should have only skeletal staffs . . . ," no new board bureaucracies. Point four recommended monthly meetings between IBHE staff and all the presidents. Point five suggested desirable new powers by the IBHE "to provide appropriate oversight and statewide perspective" to governance, and "if the institutions fail to adhere to the guidelines, the state then should consider strengthening the authority of the IBHE to eliminate academic programs no longer economically or academically justified or viable." Further, "the Board should have a role in and be kept informed of all functions of the governing boards involving state funds such as bond issues, labor negotiations, contracts and leases, and staffing levels." Point six called for making the elected U of I board appointive. Point seven called for "only public members" on the IBHE, thereby to reduce conflicts of interest by those also on system or university boards. The final exhortation of the report asserted: "This reorganization is only the beginning in making our system more efficient and effective. Universities with additional autonomy must now prove they can be responsible and creative. They should place a renewed emphasis on providing quality undergraduate education, equal opportunities for students as well as employees, and innovative strategies to offer access to a post-secondary education with minimal administrative support."

The structural and governance changes recommended were quite explicit, but the goals and rationale were pretty vague and Reagan-like. In Kustra's interview, he responded with the highlights of the policy goals in view:

> Well, I think the first one is accountability. I think that the ability to hold the individual institutions accountable again to those who are elected to office, to those who pay tuition, is more difficult when you have this centralized bureaucracy in Springfield that was removed from either the elected leadership of the state or the folks back on the campuses or those back home who were paying the bills. That is the most important one. We are really trying to give the power back to those most directly affected. As one who served as a faculty member at one of the universities under the Board of Regents, Sangamon State University, I must say that another goal that drove this in my own mind was to deal with the arrogance of university administration in general. I don't understand how this happens in a system that is supposed to operate so democratically and so collegially, but unfortunately university administration tends to get so far removed from the rest of the world. They operate in their own cocoons. They simply don't have their ear to the ground. I have seen this in too many cases across Illinois. Almost every one of the university presidents over the last few years came to me with examples of how this was the case.

Later, he added a comment on the effect of greater authority in the IBHE for oversight:

> Will these powers cause the schools to become more alike? I'd say no more alike than they can be by the current system. I think we're leaving everything in place, and even with these new powers, the system will probably look pretty similar to the way it is now. By 2020, I think, there will be some benefits to students who can gain better access to their governing boards. I think parents who pay tuition can be reassured that we're serious about cost effective administrations, holding down the size of administrations so the money goes into the classroom. Whatever happens by 2020, it's not going to be adversely affected by this bill. Instead it will be marginally improved by downsizing administration, centralization, and getting the money down into the classroom.

Near the end of his comments, Kustra added the personal dimension: "As I said earlier, I just think there was an arrogance about these two agencies and their chancellors that rubbed many legislators the wrong way over the years. And I just happened to be one of them who achieved a position to do something about it."

Kirk Dillard, Republican sponsor in the Senate, for the restructure legislation, elaborated the expected outcomes somewhat differently:

> Well, the most important one I think is greater accountability for students, their parents, local residents or business owners, and faculty and staff. All will have better access to whomever their board of trustees would be. One of the things that the bill does is put the board of trustees on campus for public meetings more often than the current system does. If I have a student in school and I'm a parent, I will know how to get ahold of the board. It's just a much closer entity to the user of the institution and the local geographic area. For the regional institutions, it brings the decision making and the accountability much closer to the users or neighbors of that institution. I know that this bill will save some money in terms of fiscal cost. It's debatable how much, but that was a concern as well. So it's accountability coupled with a little bit of administrative cost savings. And the final one, not one that the governor really talked much about—but I believe as the sponsor of this bill that overall we will be able to recruit a better stock of candidates for the boards. People from business, from labor, from academia, or from communities can serve on the university boards. When I worked for Jim Thompson and Jim Edgar, I would make calls to see if people were interested in serving on the Board of Regents or the Board of Governors. Oftentimes, a business person would tell me, "I would love to serve on this board, but I don't have the time away from my business to travel to five different schools for the Board of Governors and three different ones for the Board of Regents." Oftentimes somebody may have an interest in higher education and a specific institution. But they might not have a great interest in the other two or three institutions. These people turned us down. So overall I think you're going to get a very high quality person to serve on the new boards. You'll have more people coming forward who might not have the time to serve or want to do the travel under the old arrangements. It's not so much the time; it's the travel for certain boards. And I think overall higher ed will be better off in terms of the overall capacity to have better decision makers, a wider brush of decision makers, than we have now.

*Van Der Slik:* The bills that already passed and are signed, do they go far enough?

*Dillard:* I think they go far enough now. The Board of Higher Ed is coming around wanting some additional authority especially to keep tuition equalized. But I think the less power the IBHE has, the better. Again, we wanted greater local accountability for each institution. And I don't want the IBHE to come in and suck up much of the authority that we've given these individual boards for each university. So the less power the Board of Higher Education has, the better. Will there have to be fine tuning? Perhaps, but I think this bill has just gone far enough, and I'm not sure we ought to actually start picking it apart yet until we see how it works.

For Art Quern, IBHE chair and cochair of the task force, the emphasis was always on accountability:

> Since I have taken this job, I've always believed that the public is willing to support programs and activities of government that they think serve a good purpose and are accountable for the performance. [University administrators] must execute in serving that purpose. Then I felt that higher education didn't take its accountability seriously. They thought they were perceived to be a good and an obvious good. Why would anybody ask them to be accountable? Then there's issues of academic freedom. But I think that the more accountable people perceive higher education to be, the better chance you have to getting the fair share of what's available from the taxpayers. I think last year's budget request, which was a tempered request, but not insignificant, was fully responded to by the governor and the General Assembly. I think we'll get a good response this year because they feel with PQP we've really tried to be accountable. We've gotten an indication that demonstrating accountability and a concern with how the $2 billion are spent, not just how much more are we going to get in incremental pieces, is the best way to argue and win for higher education. To the extent that the new players in the rearranged structure understand and support this question of accountability, it will be better. If they fail to, they can fail under this structure just as did under the old structure. If they fail, they'll lose ground with the public. There is no longer automatic reverence for higher education that may have existed earlier. There is even an economic question. People are saying what I used to say: "If you got a degree from institution x, that means your going to earn a million dollars more in your life. And that's why institution x is so much more expensive." Well, those don't quite hold up any longer. So people are saying, "I'm spending all this money and the price is increasing, but I'm not sure I personally get the economic payback." So the kind of reverence for the institutions and the economic clarity that people viewed as the benefit have been blurred. So higher education has to work at demonstrating, dealing with change, trying to meet the needs of the future and be accountable for the university. To that extent it will be relatively well-funded in the scheme of public funding. That's where I come from on this.

For Quern, however, the highest priority was in adding to the oversight powers of the IBHE. With PQP, the IBHE had, in Quern's view, proved its capability and would, with sterner oversight powers, make the universities leaner and more effective:

> The point here is we believe that there should be a board outside the institution itself which oversees certain key issues, those issues that we think have to do with tuition policy, capital projects, and programs. What we're saying is that if you devolve some of the responsibilities of governing to the seven boards,

we would suggest that in order to have proper accountability and oversight on behalf of the taxpayers overall that you ask the Board of Higher Education to review tuition and approve tuition increases, that you ask the Board of Higher Education to review and approve capital requests, that you ask the Board of Higher Education to have the ability to eliminate programs, that we grant the power to the Board of Higher Education to eliminate programs as well as approve new ones. Our thinking is rather straight forward. In terms of tuition policy, there really has to be someplace where consistency in approaching tuition should be the concern. Every campus which gets its own board is naturally going to say, "We need more money. The professors aren't paid well enough. Some faculty need more equipment, and the state's not providing enough assistance. We've got to raise tuition." Well, you could get one school raising tuition 75 percent and another raising it 10 percent and one student in one part of the state paying that lower cost for the same program that somebody else in the other part of the state is paying for at a higher rate. You really need to have some review that says there is some consistency here and also some constraint. You need an outside power for constraint. We think that for tuition policy that is clear and obvious. Capital—the concern there is that somebody other than an institution should have the ability to approve or disapprove—it's very easy for an institution to get enamored of a particular project, to find a donor, or someone who's going to help fund it. Suddenly, a foundation or some contributor has built this new building, and then they turn to the state and say, "Okay, now we need the operating money." That's a foolish way to go. We think there needs to be an outside review which says, "Before you get into deciding about any capital, let's see what your program is, why do you need that building, how you are going to operate, where is the money going to come from?" That has to be asked by somebody outside the institution. I believed for a long time that unless the Board of Higher Education has the power to eliminate programs, very few programs will ever get eliminated because it's the natural posture of any campus to say, "Hey, these are good programs, these people are tenured, and they did a good job. We want to offer it to the students in this geography. And maybe it's not quite the quality that we'd like, but we don't want to eliminate it." My own concern is that leads to a gradual dilution of all quality, because what happens instead of eliminating low quality, lesser important programs, you keep them limping along, and you take a little bit of money from something that's a high priority. You don't give it quite as much as you would have. So the high priority program doesn't get as much; it suffers. And the low priority doesn't get very much, but it gets a little, and it suffers. So overall quality is brought down. I think that's a natural tendency. Business found that everywhere. You really needed a force that put on to the agenda a real question about what are your priorities. Then make choices amongst those priorities. That's why the IBHE should have that power.

Even among the prime movers, there were widely differing expectations about outcomes and the relationship between the means chosen to move the system and what was to be accomplished.

Observers, including some of the major players, were puzzled by the vague rationale for such a broad range of proposals. Ikenberry indicated he had early correspondence with Kustra about the original task force report:

> First, I was not convinced at that time that a rational case had been made to reorganize higher organization in the state. It wasn't clear to me that there was any obvious rationale or purpose underlying the various recommendations. And I was concerned at that time that it might lead to undue fragmentation within the higher education system. And I did register those concerns. I think as I continued to work with it, while I continued to have many of those concerns, it also seemed to me that the rationale behind the reorganization became clear. Namely, that people did honestly feel, from a philosophical standpoint, that moving the governance and the decision making closer to the campus for many of these state universities would be a step forward. It would help reduce the bureaucracy, that it would give better oversight and perhaps better advocacy to the individual campuses. I think now what we need to do is do everything we can do to make the system work as comfortably as possible and let the verdict of history, which will come down to us, say whether this was a wise move or not.

Ikenberry did not accept the rationale, however, he accepted the sincerity of those who put it forward. But that was on the decentralization and changing his own board to an appointive one. He vigorously and successfully disarmed and defeated the notion of strengthening IBHE oversight.

Chancellor Layzell, of the BOG system, observed: "On a couple of occasions, Bob Kustra noted that the reason they didn't include SIU and U of I was essentially the political reason that they felt that it would be too difficult to accomplish. One of the points that I made, particularly two years ago, was if this is such a good idea for seven schools, why is it not a good idea for all twelve? They just didn't think politically they could push that change even though you might recognize there is some logic to it." Rod Groves, at the regency system, likewise sensed the political vulnerability of BOR and BOG. He dismissed the task force for its lack of substance: "They were more of a cheering section for Bob Kustra."

Samuel Gove, a participant observer in the evolution of the system of systems, was surprised by the meagerness of the task force activities:

> I was kind of shocked the way the Kustra commission was put together, the task force. One of my friends from the University was on it, Jane Hayes Rayder. If you questioned her, she would probably tell you they hardly met. It was a foregone conclusion that separate boards was the way they wanted to go. Of course, the unhappiness of Eastern with the Board of Governors precipitated

all of this. I was shocked there was no attempt to have any serious hearings. I was shocked there was no research. The earlier reorganization committees [during the 1960s] were very thorough. I guess there really hasn't been any since the master plan, but then there was considerable consensus building and research studies. I couldn't believe this, but in the background, you have to remember that as very young legislators, two former interns, Jim Edgar and Doug Kane, fooled around with higher education reorganization, and they got a lot of mileage and press on it, but they never introduced a bill.

An articulate critic, House Democrat Barbara Currie, looked at the case for hastily conceived change and found none:

The proponents of the change never made a good educational case for the change. While certainly one could complain about this or that aspect of the way we organize higher education, no one has made a cogent argument that the system was indeed badly broken and in need of a major fix. If there were some major problems with the current system, there ought to have been a look, a careful look, at the way things are structured in other states, states like Wisconsin or California. One alternative is a single state university, the University of Illinois, with branches at Macomb, at Charleston, and so forth. So I never had the impression that there was a really careful look at completely different ways of structuring higher education. And as I say, I'm not holding out for anything magical in our way of doing business. It's just that no one ever made a case that convinced me that the system was badly broken. And when it came to an alternative way of doing business, I certainly think that we did not pay adequate attention to alternative forms of organization. The one the lieutenant governor chose seems to me to be unsatisfactory in that it may increase the vulnerability of particular institutions, and it may invite the legislature to act as a super school board, which is hardly what I would think of as good for educational policy.

She offered her analysis this way:

However, in my opinion, if your interest is in trying to improve the quality of public higher education, if your interest is in trying to rationalize the system of public higher education, this doesn't do it. This is superficial. It isn't going to help meet either of those two goals. And no one made the argument that it would. No one could make a sensible argument that says that this will create a better, a more efficient, a more rational, or a higher quality outcome than the current system. So it's a funny way for Quern to go if he was the person behind it. I could imagine that he, along with Wagner, would be interested in beefing up IBHE, and that might be harder to accomplish if you've got two subsidiary boards. But I would think all of these institutions set up on their own will make life tougher for IBHE. It's going to be tougher for IBHE to retain credibility, to be the kind of player that it's been in the past. So again, I envision individual legislators and individual caucuses and all kinds of politics coming to the fore. If you want to rationalize programs and you don't want to offer a zillion programs at all these different institutions, well, you know, you saw what happened with the law school at Northern. And I would imagine that there will be more of that. Now what coalitions will form in order to be able for that to happen, who knows?

The end result was not a very tidy legislative package. According to Phil Adams: "The current act is sloppy. They pushed this thing through rapidly, and I understand why they did. Their feeling is we have the house, we have the senate. If we need to tinker with it later, we've got the votes to do something. It's probably true. But they passed it so rapidly that there are problems. One of the problems is that they didn't know how to handle the membership of the board of higher education."

To the disappointment of the IBHE and especially its chair, Art Quern, the enlargement of IBHE powers never was even introduced as a bill in 1995. Art Quern had wanted the IBHE powers put into the restructure bill. However, tactics were in the hands of the governor and lieutenant governor, who decided that the appointive board for the U of I and the IBHE powers would be in separate bills. Richard Wagner made the case for added IBHE powers. Nothing united the higher education community in 1995 more than that proposal. Ikenberry blasted it with a letter to Wagner that had copies going to numerous players. Garrett Deakin, SIU's liaison, was negative when I asked about more powers for the IBHE. Asked if it would pass, he said: "No! They went to the House, they talked to 22 people, and nobody would take it! They went to the Senate, they talked to the current Senate sponsors, half a dozen to a dozen Senate sponsors, nobody would take it." Representative Wirsing confirmed the point, quoting an unnamed Republican member who said, "I was elated that the governor's office called me, but I looked at it and said I can't sponsor that." The chilly reception in the legislature "really sent a message to the governor's office, sent a message to the IBHE, and sent a message between the colleges as well." According to Ross Hodel, deputy director of the IBHE, the sharp reaction from Ikenberry and the presidents at NIU, ISU, and EIU caught the governor and his legislative supporters by surprise. From the vantage point of the House Republication leadership, Tom Ryder's comment is informative:

> In a way, the state Board of Higher Education was put in the same posture as the Board of Governors and Board of Regents, as a layer of bureaucracy. At the end of the decision-making process to get rid of a layer of bureaucracy, there was a feeling to do more—I'm trying to think of some management terms here—to put the management at the site. Meaning let Northern run its show and have less responsibilities to the state Board of Higher Education. So I think that part of the process of getting rid of bureaucracy meant that we didn't

want to add to a bureaucracy, and we also felt that in that vacuum, an attempt by higher ed [IBHE] to grab some more, to get some power, just wasn't well received. It didn't have the same kind of credibility or expectations. They were kind of put in the same category as those we were trying to eliminate.

The rationale for restructuring, particularly as a decentralizing action, did not carry with it a compelling argument for granting greater authority to the IBHE, a central bureaucracy. Making all of the boards, including the U of I board, appointive was accomplished. But contrary to the governor, Quern, and IBHE, legislators were willing to allow the community college system to be pulled out from under the IBHE's oversight. The legislature pushed the decision up to the governor, who vetoed it and persuaded its sponsors not to go for an override. Ross Hodel, IBHE's legislative liaison, said, "I have never worked so long and hard in a General Assembly session and produced such a lack of positive results." A mixed blessing was that the governor proposed a very positive budget for the universities. However, because universities were getting financial resources easily, they did not have to present a united front. "That removed one common element that usually binds us together. . . ." Hodel went on to say:

> Certainly, the whole governance question began this, and then I think our reaction, our response, to the governance issue unleashed a whole myriad of things. Our board was relatively neutral on the whole topic of governance. Then it agreed to request additional powers. So really we were friends to no one during the legislative session. The Board of Regents and Board of Governors felt we had abandoned them. They felt we were conspiring with the governor. Legislative staff and governor's staff felt there was really only one higher ed issue for them this year. That was the governance restructuring, and IBHE was sort of neutral on that topic. We really weren't with them as strongly and as effectively as they thought we should have been. With regard to the extra powers, the violent reaction really caught them by surprise.

## Conclusion

Not unlike American national politics, Illinois policy-making occurs in a complex partisan environment. The Illinois agenda orientation changed with the economy and the electoral outcomes. In the first legislative session, the agenda orientation was contracting and fiscally restrictive. It remained contractive in 1993, although the governor sought to move higher education changes. Success was limited to the Senate. After the election in 1994, the state was escaping fiscal constraints, and the governor and Republican legislative leaders agreed to a significant list of policy actions and a fast-track strategy. Higher education restructuring was on that list, along with making the U of I board appointive. Fast and positive action carried the day in early 1995.

It is fair to say that the restructuring fits Jones's notions of ambitious decision-making leading to speculative augmentation. The policy qualifies as a substantial, if not earthshaking, change. But its theoretical rationale was thin. It could be rationalized by its proponents, but even its advocates did not fully agree about what they were trying to achieve or what would constitute evidence of accomplishment. Its opponents acknowledged that its enactment was certain but could criticize the inconsistencies of the actual proposals along with its thin rationale.

The policy changes that have been adopted will not likely soon be reversed. There is a new shape to the higher education reality in Illinois that is very likely beyond partisan change until a new premise for change makes its way on to the scene. The separate identities for seven different universities can now be better established and nurtured in their different locations and with their distinctive alumni. They will make their way only modestly coordinated by an IBHE that did not get enhanced coordinating powers. Representative Weaver, a Republican, dismissed that as a "power grab"—not necessarily a wrong one, but one he would certainly oppose. The two big systems, U of I and SIU, are unlikely to change their antipathy to greater IBHE coordination. If seven other universities thrive in their separateness, they too will resist external coordination.

Two of the less passionate respondents saw future results to be shaped less by policy shifts than marketplace pressures. Representative Tom Ryder put his trust in "the market": "I think competition for students and students to have choices are important . . . [and] changing the boards does not change the competition for students much." Paula Wolff, president of Governors State, carried the point further: "I think whether or not [the policy changes] are good for Illinois will be a function of whether or not the various institutions that now will have more autonomy or less autonomy can thrive in a competitive higher education environment. I believe that competition among institutions is probably a very good and sound way to promote educational quality. So I think in the long run probably it is good."

Present in the political context of this study is an element not anticipated in Jones's study of presidential transitions. He did not look for or take note of presidents whose mandate improved markedly in the second term. There were none among the six presidents and five transitions that he examined. But in Illinois, Jim Edgar entered the governorship with a slim majority, inheriting a low congruity policy agenda, a low turnover legislature controlled by the opposition party, and a crushing budgetary shortfall. But his reelection, along with House and Senate majorities for his party in 1994 and a rise in economic well-being for the state, made major policy accomplishments attainable. Legislative membership changed, and new Republicans were amenable to policy changes, including the higher education restructure. A strong measure of agenda continuity was achieved, setting up the possibility for ambitious decision-making and speculative augmentation. This phenomenon, unanticipated in Jones's work, may be looked for in earlier presidencies as well as among other elected executives in states and cities.

# 6 | Dimensions of Conflict and Policy Images

A novel approach to policy-making analysis has emerged in the last decade that brings attention to "policy punctuation." Jones, Baumgartner, and True (1998) argue that in particular subsystems, there are periods of grid-lock and periods of dramatic change. The periods of stability may be long and the periods of change brief. However, incrementation fails, and change breaks out instead.

> Such punctuations are an important part of policy making even if most policies most of the time are subject to no such dramatic events. Rather than making adaptive adjustments to an ever-changing environment, political decision making is characterized by stasis, when existing decision designs are routinely employed, and sometimes by punctuation, when a slowly growing condition suddenly bursts onto the agendas of a new set of policy makers, or when existing decision makers shift attention to new attributes or dimensions of an existing situation. (2)

It can reasonably be argued that Illinois' higher education system of systems was put together in 1957 to 1967 in a series of events including the formation of the board of higher education and its first two master plans (Matsler and Hines 1987). Legislation passed in 1967 created the Board of Regents, created two new upper-division universities, Sangamon State and Governors State, and recognized two Chicago schools, Chicago State and Northeastern, in the statute. After that, operations did indeed go forward with little other than incremental change. The master plans of 1971 and 1976 acknowledged and accepted the continuing desirability of the system of systems, with coordinated planning at the top from the IBHE. Thereafter, requests for new programs, budgets, and buildings usually welled up from the campuses and campus administrators, went through system review, and then when through system of systems (IBHE) review. Within and across systems, faculty and administrators kept wary eyes upon one another. Fairness and equity were often argued. The interpretation that the system of systems incorporated appropriate checks and balances was widely accepted.

## Old and New Dimensions of Conflict

When the IBHE received a report of its Committee on Scope, Structure, and Productivity in March 1990, the report called on the board to enlarge access for students, improve the quality of undergraduate education, and increase productivity. These were politically correct requests from a largely education establishment study committee. Moreover, the committee found "no compelling reason to change the existing organizational structure of Illinois higher education" (Illinois Board of Higher Education 1990). The system of systems was doing well, but could do better.

*Old Dimensions*

The conflicts in the system of systems were mostly ⌐bout budget. The issues were subsumed by the subtitle of Harold Lasswell's famous 1936 work, *Who Gets What, When, How.* When Rod Groves, BOR chancellor, was asked what brought about the restructuring, he attributed it to stress within the system over the enduring question of resources:

> I would have to say the root cause is the chronic under funding of higher education and the disappointments that has engendered, particularly at the institutional level in Illinois higher education. What that has tended to do is to generate frustration which has focused on structure and advocacy and the apparent inadequacy of that in the campus perspective. Those frustrations or those disappointments over the last 30 years have led people to be frustrated and to feel that there has to be a better way and to look for a better way. It started in the first instance when the system of systems was created. Higher education is overwhelmingly popular, and people on the campuses know it. Students out there want higher education. Their parents want higher education. You just don't hear long speeches about how ghastly higher education is. You don't hear the kind of negative discussions with regard to higher education that you hear about the state's human services, for example. Higher education is very popular and has always been very popular, and so the campuses are aware of that. Naturally, they think in terms of making those opportunities more broadly available. But the money isn't there. The support isn't there. Why are these people in the legislature not providing us that money? Well, one answer might be because they have a restraint on them—the taxpayers. But from the perspective of the campuses, an equally plausible explanation is because they have such inadequate advocacy in their behalf. So this tended to be, it seems to me, the underlying condition which has motivated the whole reorganization.

Groves's ability to identify the old problem of resources along with the deficiencies of advocacy in behalf of higher education fits a larger, national picture. Darryl G. Greer (1986, 27) identified that same dilemma as the inherent problem for higher education coordinating boards. The political branches view educational coordinating boards as regulatory. But the universities and the people in them regard such bodies as the ones to advocate their needs and aspirations.

Despite the old problem of money, many of the players in and around the system were comfortable with it. Delores Cross, president at Chicago State, was the senior president in the BOG system when I interviewed her:

> Well, initially looking at it, I was very comfortable with being a part of a system because at one point [in my career] I was vice chancellor of the City University of New York. I have had the system experience. So I was really comfortable with that notion. . . .

*Van Der Slik:* Do you feel that the dissolution of the Board of Governors was good for Chicago State or not?

*Cross:* Well, I flip flop on that. It has been my experience that just given the uniqueness of Chicago State University that it's been really difficult to get an adequate response to the needs that the institution has. Chicago State serves a very different population than other schools do, but we are constantly being compared with the other four schools. Indeed, when resources were needed for Chicago State University, the System was always weighted with downstate concerns. So now there is some advantage in our being able to articulate to our own board what our needs are without feeling the frustration of those old comparisons. "Okay you are doing really well; we recognize your needs, but there are four other universities." Now we don't hear as much about four other universities within that system configuration, but I know that we are going to hear that within state configurations, you know, there are 11 other public universities. We may have just changed the configuration rather than the reality of experiences with comparison.

Cross anticipates the old dimension of conflict over money will simply be reconfigured with more individualized contestants in the future.

Richard Wagner, the IBHE executive director, continues to see his role in coordination. I asked, "If you were Czar, how would you respond to the proposed changes?"

> Well, I'm not Czar. I am not. I'm executive director of the Board of Higher Education. The Board of Higher Education has a major role to play in the planning and coordination of higher education. We need very definitely to work as effectively as we can within the structure of higher education as determined by the governor and General Assembly. I'm going to focus my efforts on making the system work whatever the structure is. The system we had for the university governance was a system of four system boards governing twelve campuses. We're now going to two system boards governing five campuses and then seven campus boards. Theoretically, the system governing board is separate from the campus. There is in essence a check and balance built in. But in a campus governing board, the campus and the governing board are one and the

same. Therefore, you need to provide some checks and balances elsewhere in the system. Look at Illinois State. A very effective and strong president has been able to work with a foundation board to supplement his salary. Where was the check and balance? The check and balance was there in the Board of Regents, but it failed. So that illustrates the oversight issue. I know that the campuses have said, "Power grab, power grab." I said that the three things I've consistently heard during my years as executive director is that one, faculty morale has never been lower. Number two, more money will solve the problem. And number three, IBHE's actions are a power grab. So, you know, come on, come on friends. Let's get real. These are very legitimate public policy questions, and they merit more discussion than they have received.

According to Wagner, the existing tensions within the system of systems were what kept checks and balances working most of the time. Failures called for improvement in performance, not major structural change to the system. But if such changes were to come, he believed he needed more authority for the top board to keep the now larger number of independent schools in coordination.

Political defenders of the old system were also comfortable with the way it worked. Representative Currie wanted it to keep working that way, ending on the point of spending decisions and why they shouldn't become a matter of legislative particularism:

My particular concern is with the newer, more vulnerable institutions and those that either have a special mission or tend to deal with particular kinds of students, minority students, for example. I think the present structure provides some protection to those institutions. Others in the system, like Northern Illinois University and the University of Illinois, have avid and active alumni organizations. Newer institutions like Chicago State University don't. I think that the BOR and BOG systems have helped to sort things out and even out the playing field. The effect of that has been not only to protect the more vulnerable newer institutions but it's also been to keep the legislature from acting like an enlarged school board. From time to time issues that are of concern to a particular institution do come before us, in effect sidestepping the systems and Board of Higher Education, but it happens rarely. I think that from the policy perspective, we are better served if the legislature plays an overall policy making role rather than making determinations about whether NIU ought or ought not have a law school or whether this degree granting program ought to be available at institution X, Y, or Z. In the context of appropriations, there should be a firm mechanism in place to make some initial spending decisions without asking us to act like a super school board.

For Representative Art Turner, whose primary task was to look out for African-American interests in the system of systems, the whole idea of restructuring was not seen as helpful. He liked the game he knew better than any pie-in-the-sky proposals:

> I've kind of gotten used to dealing with the system of systems as a whole. Although there was an element of control removed from each institution, I think—at least in terms of budget concerns and for the overall picture of higher ed in the state—the system of systems was a good approach. That is true because the system of systems has never allowed it to take a very dynamic leadership role. It was just sort of the clearinghouse. But in terms of being proactive, I've never picked that up from IBHE or picked it up as them assuming that to be their role. So I always felt that the Board of Regents and Board of Governors were systems that worked. One thing that I did know was that the schools who were under the BOG, particularly those schools in the city on Chicago, I thought they stood a fighting chance because of that relationship and nature of being hooked up with downstate schools. So I was adamantly opposed to breaking up the Board of Governors. . . . I think what its going to do is polarize higher ed in the state.

Currie knew the arguments of the other side but did not see the evidence for their case:

> It was one of those odd issues that kind of popped full blown from the brain of the lieutenant governor. And as I say, all these rumors about what really brought it about were intriguing but never confirmed. If you start with scandals or obvious administrative inefficiencies or obvious unfairnesses in the system, then I would understand. If things were beginning to boil over in institution after institution, suffering under the control of the intermediate board, then I could understand where it came from. But I don't think that's the reality. And I certainly think the lieutenant governor's proposal was hastily conceived. Certainly, nobody looked at alternative ways that apparently have served other states well. It may be this was just a way to put a feather in Bob Kustra's cap, one more thirty-second sound bite in the next political campaign. I find the whole thing very peculiar.

The defenders of the system of systems were generally content to keep a balance among the schools and argue for incremental improvements in higher education funding. There was a procedure for universities to articulate their needs, but for the most part, the budget process added increments to the base, with occasional new money for especially well-justified new program initiatives.

## New Dimensions

Perhaps the key word in the restructuring argument was "accountability." But instead of accountability upward in a multilayered bureaucratic hierarchy, the accountability in the unbuttoned systems would be to gubernatorially appointed boards. Kustra put the issue in populist terms: "We are really trying to give the power back to those most directly affected." The arrogance of the costly bureaucracy was most conspicuous for Kustra in the Board of Regents and Board of Governors:

> And I think that grew over the years. First they were executive directors, then they had to be named chancellors. Then they needed bigger offices and bigger staffs. So they hired deputy chancellors and vice chancellors. Their salaries were escalated to give them the power they claimed they needed. Their salaries had to be larger than the salary of the university presidents. It's a system that just got out of control. There weren't that many people across the state of Illinois who were watching, but to those in the legislature or, in my case, in the office of lieutenant governor, I really felt like our policies were hypocritical. We were boosting up tuition, telling students that this had to occur in order for us to deliver a cost effective product. But right there at the top, the people that were overseeing this whole system were walking away with salaries that didn't need to be paid, with offices and staffs that they really didn't need. You could return all that power and decision making back to the campus level.

Representative Wirsing could see the benefits of accountability in the schools dealing with regional issues of their particular locations:

> The key achievement is clarifying accountability. The Board of Regents, the Board of Governors, IBHE—all blamed each other at times. It is not our fault; its the Regents; it is their fault. So that is gone. So I think there is an accountability now, because each of those universities have their own Board of Trustees. That Board of Trustees is going to have to set the policy for its administration; it's going to have to make some decisions like Illinois State—hiring a new president instead of interim personnel. I believe that given some time, it will allow the universities to truly deal first of all with the region that they serve. Under the old system, they were directed by people not from their region, at least those seven schools under the two governing boards. Now everybody is on the same playing field; everybody will have their own governing board— Governors State, Chicago State, and Northeastern aside—basically serve a very dense population of a region. That's their marketing pool. All of the other schools have regional issues to deal with and to serve. Some of those are very specific and very different from other regions of the state. But by the same token, they all service statewide; they all draw students from across the state. So they move beyond their region, and they have to recognize that. I think with their own Board of Trustees, that they can really address those issues.

The perception of improvement through decentralization and greater localization of control resonated with Democrats as well as Republicans. Would individual boards be a positive improvement? From the Senate Democratic leadership, Vince Demuzio took the affirmative. "I think so. The cliché is 'too much concentration in Springfield.' The Board of Higher Education functioning through the Board of Regents and the Board of Governors has had absolute control over what happens at the university system level. I think returning some local control is good. Universities should be able to administer the respective rules, regulations, laws passed by the General Assembly and developed by the legislature and the Board of Higher Ed. I think they would be better implemented at the local level."

President Ikenberry could explain the management challenge, while opposing strong statewide coordination from the IBHE:

> I think if all of higher education were brought together under one administration, it becomes very, very difficult to manage. The University of Illinois as it now exists is a very considerable management challenge. So I do not think it would be a step forward to create a super board in this state. And that's why it was with some caution I supported, ultimately supported, the Governor's reorganization that we now have. If anything, instead of creating more and more centralized planning and coordinating and governing mechanisms, we probably ought to be experimenting with decentralization of decision making. And that's basically what the new plan tries to do.

At Northern, with its long stymied aspirations for independence, President La Tourette could see the opportunity in the deregulatory mood of Republican legislators:

> The time was ripe in the BOR, because you had inherent instability, inherent tension, and dysfunctionality within the system. The BOR was a system which should have been viewed as evolving toward a breakup. Beyond the inherent conditions justifying change, the existence of a Republican legislature with a strong commitment to deregulation gave us the political basis for the deregulation of higher education. I think the break-up was easy once you had the appropriate leadership in the governor's office and legislature. A rational decision crying for a response was joined by a political philosophy and platform. All the elements had come together.
>
> Just a number of things came together in 1995 with the governor and the Republican majority holding a general commitment to deregulation and decentralization. Add to this the platform of the Republicans to moving decision making back to the customer; it's all in this mix of deregulation and letting the client, rather than government, decide. The governor had been displeased with the BOG system since he was president of the student association at Eastern. Then, in the 1990s, there was a major change in the political environment in the country. Republicans were coming into the Congress and state legislatures and carrying with them a new philosophy of government—decentralization and local control.

So the issue discussions moved away from checks and balances and increasing the equitably distributed resources to an emphasis on accountability and local control, deregulation, and letting the universities respond to the interests of their customers—students and their parents.

## Decentralization and the IBHE

In place of the image of a complex, balanced, widely distributed but increasingly costly system of systems providing accessible and broadly valued educational change to students, new and contrasting images were offered. Two softening-up articles, as Kingdon uses the term (1984, 134–38), were in prominent places. *Crain's Chicago Business* (Coleman 1992) carried the message to corporate readers that the state's universities were lagging on downsizing, disregarding bureaucratic growth, and spending needlessly on duplicative programs. Worst of all, the system was rewarding "educrats" at the expense of students. It was the views of Kustra and Quern that the article quoted favorably, including the notion that corporate-type analysis should be applied with discipline. Similarly, a prominent series in the *Chicago Tribune* by Grossman, Jouzaitis, and Leroux (1992), running four days, emphasized "how higher education as a whole, using the University of Illinois as an example, has turned away from its mission to teach undergraduate students" (21 June). The imagery was about an uncaring bureaucracy serving narrowly focused scholarship at the expense of good teaching and needs of undergraduates. By the conclusion of the series, the authors quoted Art Quern's corporate outlook: "American business is trying to rise to the challenge of doing what it does best, not always wanting to conglomerate like it did in the '80s, trying instead to eliminate unnecessary levels of management. Higher education has to start doing some of these things before it is forced to do them."

The timing on these pieces was pretty good for Kustra, the change entrepreneur. The first piece came a week before the first task force report, and the *Tribune* series came a week after.

By the time of my interviews, the language of discussion had changed. Kustra could speak easily about "downsizing administration," "getting money down into the classroom," and eliminating "the middle man," namely, system bureaucracies. He criticized a public relations contract to "create a logo for the Board of Governors. That is in addition to logos for each of the schools which they have had for years." To him that verified administrative bloat and misplaced priorities. The governor's spokesperson, Mike Lawrence, brought up the overweening interest in symbolism at the BOG and BOR:

> The Board of Governors, for example, insisted at one point that the insignia of the Board of Governors be on the football uniforms of the member's schools. I mean that's silly. That's a little thing, but I think to people who have an inclination to think, there's an extra layer of government involved here, that becomes emblematic, if you will. The emblem became emblematic. There's also

the idea that when top administrators at some of these schools were going to give a speech, they had to clear it with the governing boards. And then you look at the salaries and you look at the kind of—was it the Board of Regents that moved in to a really expensive location? It was either the Board of Regents or the Board of Governors. I mean, they didn't help themselves. They gave anecdotal material to the opponents of the system. They just handed them anecdotal material. And as you know, many times anecdotal material is more valuable than all the studies and facts. I mean, Ronald Reagan proved that.

Senator Kirk Dillard, himself a graduate of WIU and once a student member on the Board of Governors, could credibly characterize the BOG as "a strange mix of five institutions . . . a system I think is dysfunctional."

Even the opponents of the change had to acknowledge the vulnerability of the existing framework in the sense that its imagery was deficient. Democratic staffer Everson commented: "People looked at the multi-campus systems and said these are just a hodgepodge of thrown together universities. What does Charleston have to do with Chicago area universities?" When I asked Everson if his boss, Democratic Speaker Madigan, had ever gone into the fray to defend the status quo, he replied:

No, because to be honest, when the argument is phrased in the right manner, it was pretty hard to oppose. The weeding out of bureaucrats sounds good. This is not a criticism of them, but if you ever saw former Chancellors Rod Groves and Tom Layzell on TV, they were bureaucrats. At hearings, Kustra would start talking about how much money these guys and their staffs made, and everybody would just kind of cringe. This can't sound good to your average person. The average salaries at those two places were around $50,000, I would say, and chancellors were making six figures. So from a popular standpoint, it was really a tough thing to oppose.

The image of wiping out bureaucratic bloat had much greater appeal than the concept of preserving checks and balances.

Unfortunately for the governor and particularly Art Quern, the imagery about wiping out bureaucracy also cut into the effectiveness of arguments that the IBHE itself ought to be strengthened to better coordinate the remaining three systems and now seven other freestanding universities. Quern's top priority was adding teeth to the statutory power of the IBHE. The day the restructure bill was presented, Richard Wagner, IBHE executive director, spelled out the authority Quern wanted the board and its staff to have. The six powers desired (Wagner 1995) were spelled out as follows:

1. IBHE would have to approve any tuition and fee increases.
2. IBHE would have the authority to both approve and terminate academic programs.
3. IBHE would have to approve all capital projects and their financing.

4. IBHE would require reports from all university foundations about their gift money and its uses.
5. IBHE would require that all higher education bills in the legislature receive "notes" from IBHE with regard to whether such bills are in accord with master planning and IBHE budget recommendations.
6. IBHE coordination and oversight would apply the "same decision rules" to all twelve public universities.

Quern had wanted this included in the 1995 restructure bill, but the tactics of enacting separate bills were determined in the governor's office. As noted before, after the fast-track bills were passed, the governor could not get the bill sponsored to strengthen the IBHE, so the proposal died aborning.

It is interesting to note the imagery of a very important response to the proposal about the IBHE that was made public the next day from Stanley Ikenberry (1995), the U of I's president. He charged that a strengthened IBHE would mean "centralization of decision making":

> The several proposals, in effect, come close to the creation of a super board. . . . During the extensive discussions of higher education governance issues over the last two years, I can recall no one at any time suggesting that the State of Illinois move in the direction of a super board. . . . Quite to the contrary. The essence of the current proposal . . . is to decentralize—that is to place the decision making responsibility and accountability closer to the campus level.

Ikenberry went point by point in refutation of the six powers, repeatedly using the argument that centralization was wrong and keeping decision-making close to campuses was the key to responsibility and accountability.

When Representative David Wirsing, the Republican House Higher Education Committee chair, talked about the interest in the expansion of IBHE power, he used Ikenberry's term, "super board," in the negative. He was not asked to sponsor the IBHE bill because Quern and Wagner knew he opposed it. "This one super board would become an accumulation of IBHE, Board of Regents, and Board of Governors all rolled into one." But Wirsing and his colleagues were not warm to that idea. Representative Mike Weaver perceived the IBHE move as a "power grab" that he opposed "because I absolutely don't want to see the appropriation process abrogated by the Board of Higher Education." He continued: "We want universities to be individual, to have their own missions. . . . I think we ought to proceed with that." So the prospect of the IBHE standardizing the individual schools would be to prevent distinctiveness and the ability to respond to particular regional needs.

Once the decentralization theme was out of the box and the legislative response to IBHE powers was chilly, a Senate bill passed—first the Senate and then the House—to take the community college board out from the oversight of the

IBHE. The IBHE opposed, of course, but doing so only added to its political burdens. IBHE Deputy Director Ross Hodel learned that from legislative committee leaders:

> They really thought that part of the reason the community college bill moved initially and received favorable consideration is that some of the universities thought this would be a good little distraction to keep the IBHE from getting additional powers. We would have to keep scrambling on things related to community colleges. As the community college bill emerged, we got no help at all from the university folks who probably have some concerns in terms of the future of their capital projects. For instance, once the community colleges are set free, it probably will be much more competitive for everyone. My sense is that initially everyone opposed letting the IBHE get that additional power. And then the community college bill sort of took on a life of its own—underdog mentality and personalities and quest for independence. Community colleges have a laundry list of topics that serve as annual grievances, whether it's their share of student financial aid, share of the state budget, share of capital projects.

Wirsing was sympathetic to community college requests, which, he and others believed, got short shrift from the IBHE: "IBHE was taking those and throwing them in a box and kind of shaking them and pulling them out and totally readjusting the priority of capital projects for the community colleges. They weren't doing that for the universities, but they would never let them in the door to talk with them. That's not leadership. That's being a bully. That's being a dictator. That's why Senate Bill 549 [the community college bill] occurred." For President La Tourette at NIU, the quest by IBHE for more powers at the time when deregulation of the universities was moving forward simply confirmed "that the Board of Higher Education is out of tune with the changes that have occurred and are occurring." Its legislative difficulties conveyed messages to both the board and staff of the IBHE: "I think they are beginning to appreciate . . . the fact that everything they proposed fell on deaf ears. Everything they opposed was passed. I think there is a message there."

Not himself a decisionmaker, House Democratic staffer Chris Everson made a dispassionate observation about the IBHE powers: that a clear need for them was present.

> IBHE lost big. The thing about their powers legislation is that in a rational world the powers legislation actually made sense. Maybe not every element of it, but the goal was to oversee a system that is going to be much more decentralized in 1996 than it was previously. We need more oversight powers to protect the interests of the taxpayers. That doesn't sound too farfetched, but the universities were still smarting from PQP, from PQP bonuses, and from other things. They were certainly in no mood to give up any more authority to the Board of Higher Ed than they already had previously. I don't know if IBHE

could have fashioned any type of bill that could have gone anywhere, but when they put in the ability to set tuition rates and the ability to eliminate programs, campus presidents fired back. Stan Ikenberry sends off a letter stating in plain English that he's against it. That's a pretty clear signal that this thing was not going very far.

Not surprisingly, Kustra gave a rather more bland analysis. He supported the IBHE's concept but blamed its weak reception on the staff's reputation:

I believe they are organizing a bill and that it will be introduced. I talked to Quern yesterday who asked me if he could represent my position as in favor of the general proposals in that bill. I've had a chance over the weekend to read the proposals, and I've had a chance to read Stanley Ikenberry's reaction to them. I told him, "Yes, I'm generally in support." I don't think these are inconsistent with what we've tried to do. I think there has to be some coordination and leverage at a higher level than the individual boards. The individual boards will still have considerable decision making power in the day-to-day operation of their universities. But I think taxpayers, parents, and students should be reassured that state government hasn't turned these universities loose with no controls. And the Board of Higher Education is right. They should have added authority and responsibility. Perhaps the problem with this idea is that the Board of Higher Education, with very limited power of control, has a pretty bad reputation among people at the university staff level. One of the things that the IBHE staff are going to have to do is demonstrate to the legislature that they are capable of handling the new power when the old powers they exercised come under serious question. The staff of the Board of Higher Education is not respected enough to carry out their responsibilities. And I don't understand that. Perhaps I don't know enough about the inner workings of higher education administration. But I know enough that when I go into elementary and secondary school districts and deal with faculty, in the good school districts, faculty and principals have a respect for the competency of the superintendent and staff. There is no such respect in universities across the state. And that's going to have to be dealt with. And that's why Art Quern and Dick Wagner may have more trouble getting this through than they now expect.

So for Kustra, there was no inconsistency. However, getting the powers was not to be his problem, but Quern's and Wagner's. By the end of the session, as Hodel acknowledged, "we were friends to no one." Everson agreed: "You pit everyone against the Board of Higher Ed who usually is being conciliatory to everyone. Talk about the Board of Higher Ed, they had a terrible year. Just a terrible year." Later he added, "To be honest, I think if you put a bill out on the floor this year to get rid of them, it might have passed." So the IBHE and its powers request languished. It took a gubernatorial veto to keep the community college board under the IBHE, and the staff was in a posture of needing to rebuild frayed relationships after the legislative session was adjourned.

## Appointive Board

The restructure bill provided for appointed seven-member boards for seven independent schools, but this was simply an enlargement of the preexistent system of appointing members to the system boards. One university, however, had for more than a century had an elected board. Every two years, three U of I board seats were filled through the partisan election process. With terms of six years, these offices were won by statewide election.

The nominating procedure varied from the normal way that candidates get on the primary ballot—that is, by petitioning and winning nomination through votes in the primary election. The U of I Alumni Association maintained two trustee nominating committees, one for each political party (see Nowlan, Ross, and Schwartz 1984, 17–19). The committees would interview and recommend to the state party organizations three candidates each. The Democrats, by tradition, received one nomination from the Cook County Democratic Party. Party conventions would officially nominate, usually following the alumni committee recommendations. Candidates ran at large in the state, the three highest vote getters being the winners.

Conventional wisdom in Illinois vote analyses is that in "candidate centered" races such as for governor and U.S. senator, voting variation depends a great deal on the persons and pairings of each race. But in races when candidates are not very visible personally and vote variations among those of each party are typically small, the vote is "party centered" (Monroe 1982, 159–61). In their study of U of I trustee candidates, looking mostly on nominees in 1978 and 1980, Nowlan, Ross, and Schwartz (1984) found some variations among candidates. They attributed the variations to ballot position, "friends and neighbors" support, and campaigning. They suggested the possible relevance of endorsements and cues such as gender and ethnic origin. Nevertheless, they did conclude that "using the votes for trustee candidates as a measure of general party strength appears to be reasonable under certain circumstances" but argued that "trustee candidates are less invisible than some have thought" (22).

They also found and reported that with regard to spending on campaigns, only one of twelve candidates had spent over $3,000 (that person reported $5,983). But, by 1992, one Republican candidate estimated that her spending, in a losing cause, was $30,000. That year, however, Democrats swept all three seats. In fact, Gary La Paille, state Democratic Party chair, had gone public with the idea of politicizing the trustee election and making party control a goal.

According to Phil Adams, liaison for the regency system, that helped Republicans coalesce in support of the proposal to make U of I board positions appointive: "When Gary La Paille said, 'We're going to slate our own guys and we're going to win,' I think that helped them." Democrats were threatening to disregard the convention of Alumni Association selections and simply make the nominations a strictly Democratic Party determination. For the Democratic year of 1992, with Clinton at the top of the ticket, Democrats carried all three spots at stake and controlled the board by a 6 to 3 margin. That political result was just two months before the governor's final task force report in January 1993, recommending that the board be made appointive. A bill to effectuate the change passed in the Republican dominated Senate but not in the Democrat dominated House that spring. The bill to make the change was adopted in 1995 on the fast track in the House, with 66 votes, while in the Senate, it passed with the minimum required 30 votes.

Senate sponsor Kirk Dillard discussed the reaction from U of I trustees and his rationale for the change:

> I've had calls from I'd say half the board of trustees at the U of I who don't like it. I've got to tell you, I've got great admiration for those people who will drive all over Illinois to be candidates for the Board. It's a big state. They run races for these things. With all due respect, the average voter who goes into the election booth—the bottom line is nobody knows who these people are. People say that the ballot is too long anyway. I just think with the advice and consent of the Senate overall, you're going to consistently get a very good balance of people on there. And it takes a little bit of the politics out of the U of I board because I think it will be a 5 to 4 board politically. We've seen the U of I board get a little more politicized over the last few years. I use the Paula Wolff incident at the University of Illinois at Chicago. That's where you had Richard Daley— you say some Democratic politics—Republican politics—that ran it and that shouldn't be. So there's a lot of reasons why the appointed board is the way to go. It makes the ballot shorter. With all respect to those people, no one knows who those candidates are anyway. There will be more political balance while taking a little bit of the partisanship away from the University of Illinois, which I think is good.

*Van Der Slik:* It could be argued that they lose their independence now that they're dependent on the appointment by the governor.

*Dillard:* Yes and no. Their terms are six years; the governor's term is essentially four. They're staggered terms. In the last twenty years in Illinois, we have seen only two men in the governor's office. But up until Jim Thompson, governors turned over everything pretty rapidly, so there would be autonomy if you follow the history of the state up until Jim Thompson. The governor appoints the state board of education. He appoints the other university trustees. The men on those boards are pretty independent. I've worked through three governors at least, in terms of working around the capitol. And they live pretty independently of the governor. The one exception would be when Dan Walker really pushed the Board of Governors to unionize the faculty over there. Those boards are historically not going to be bothered by the governor's office. They act pretty independently. I don't think that's a real problem. I've got to tell you, too, if you're a Republican member of the board of trustees and you're elected, you still will from time to time be subject to political pressure from the leader of your party. Jim Thompson called Susan Gravenhorst or Don Grabowski or both members. He's the governor, the leader of his party. So there's still a lot of political influence. And actually, to run for those offices, you may be a bigger political animal than one who was appointed. So I think that influence is still there. Those people are elected to do certain things, and I really think that there will be less political influence and more independence with an appointed board than an elected board. Most of those elected board members, while they want to serve the U of I, tend to come from political backgrounds. They are political people. They're good people. They're very fine trustees. But clearly they are more partisan than perhaps some independent businessman or woman or community leader that a governor would appoint or put on there.

Dillard could distinguish political balance and reduced partisanship and add the idea of getting better board leaders by appointment. Phil Adams made the point more clearly:

When the bill went through to change the U of I board from elected to appointed, which was a brilliant idea, I think most people felt that the U of I would come out and oppose that and try to kill it. In reality, it was their bill. What it does for you—

*Van Der Slik:* Yeah, tell me.

*Adams:* Great bill. Great bill. I don't know who came up with this idea. I would imagine that he would never take credit for it, but Craig Bazzani has to have been in the background here, because he thinks in these kind of terms, old Dan Walker guy. It gives you the opportunity to take a public university and make the board look a lot like a large private university. The reason it does that is that you have people in the state that are very important players. They won't mind being appointed to the U of I board, but they are certainly never going to lower themselves to run for election.

*Van Der Slik:* Say somebody from Commonwealth Edison?

*Adams:* Sam Skinner—it would not shock me to see him appointed. He's never going to run for it. But he'd be a hell of a board member. Maybe you'd get the head of Motorola. Maybe you'd get someone from the city. But it lets you get people of that caliber. Under their election process in the past, for decades it was clearly a matter of who the alumni board said it wanted. I think they had some pretty lousy members under that process.

Ross Hodel, deputy director of the IBHE, agreed, saying the governor would have a difficult but enviable power of appointment:

I have to believe that one of the toughest jobs the governor will have is choosing board members. There will be a great number of the state's establishment elite who would like to be on the U of I board of trustees. People who in the past would not have been successful going the alumni association route or the political route. But now they will see an opportunity to target their efforts.

*Van Der Slik:* Won't that make that board become more aggressive? The U of I already has half of the state's higher education resources. Isn't this likely to make them more aggressive not only for resources but also for students and also for status and national standing and all of that?

*Hodel:* Yes, I think that's one of the ways that could go, certainly. In the past, we've had a very powerful president. It would be interesting to have a very powerful board chair there. And that could be happening. Now people can name presidents back three, four, or five administrations. Very few can name trustees.

The U of I board members, of course, had stakes in this issue. Tom Lamont, chair, and elected as a Democrat, acknowledged that among U of I board members there was more interest in the board appointment proposal than the governor's idea to restructure the universities. It was a delicate matter, but Lamont's political realism told him that because it actually passed in the Senate in 1993, the Republican legislature would now enact the bill:

> The [U of I] administration had voiced its opposition to a change two years ago. There was little opportunity for that to be done this time, nor do I think there was any inclination to get too deeply involved.

*Van Der Slik:* Do you sense in any way that there was a quid pro quo? You got SSU. You accept our judgment that you ought to have an appointed board.

*Lamont:* No, I don't. I think that the administration firmly believed that a change would be healthy. No.

*Van Der Slik:* I am picking up some other perspectives about this. For example: "I think those guys were asleep at the switch when this happened. They could have stopped it if they really wanted to."

*Lamont:* I frankly doubt that. I was aware of what was going on. Part of my profession, livelihood, is to spend time at the capital and lobby. I talked to any number of people, and I never got the sense that it could be stopped, because we never had anything to offer in return. I believe the governor had made it clear to his legislative leaders that this was his interest—this being the higher ed organization, which included the change of how we select trustees—and that in return he was a strong supporter of business reforms [such as tort reform] that were going through. I do not believe he was the proponent of those business reforms. He only approved them. They were put on the agenda by the legislative leaders of his party. I do not believe he proposed those changes. But this one he had. And I believe that this might have been part of the trade off. The Republicans were pretty much locked into their position. The leadership took a position on this proposal. And they have significant power in numbers to control its outcome. If you look at the votes on those things, you'll see that it was pretty much a party line vote. So I don't know who we would have knocked off on the Republican side.

> . . . Once I knew they were serious about pushing this through, I knew it was going to happen. And so I didn't expend any personal capital, political or

otherwise, to prevent it. It was a done deal. . . . But the governor's people had done a very good job of convincing alumni and others that somehow we elected board members that were so political that we couldn't get anything done, and we were bad for the university. I think there was a general feeling out there among certain segments of people interested in the U of I that we either may not have been the caliber of people that should be running the university or that we were not independent, that we were, in fact, beholden to political parties because we were elected. Of course, this all stemmed from the past decade in which alumni-nominated board members were often pushed aside by political party nominations. And once that began to happen, then they were upset, not being part of the process. But the alumni people were pushed out of the process.

*Van Der Slik:* Therefore, they could support an appointed board better?

*Lamont:* I believe they then felt that the caliber of nominations weren't up to par or did not have the best interest of the university to heart. Therefore, we could do better. Yes, they were supportive.

President Ikenberry spoke about the change from an elective to appointive board at some length. He argued that the change was a plus, that he supported it, that it might make the board and president "more attentive to the interests and concerns of the governor," but that past gubernatorial intrusion had been minimal, so a busy governor would hardly have time or reason to micromanage the university. "The key," said Ikenberry, "will be the care the governor takes in making these appointments. Whether the governor will really be able to get a new standard for the appointments he makes, that might, in the long term, be of great benefit to the university." The personalities involved could affect the relationships, but Ikenberry saw this aspect of the higher education policy changes as a movement into the mainstream of governance: "We have to remember that the structure to which Illinois is moving is the predominant structure in American higher education. To have an elected board of trustees is what was unusual."

Ikenberry acknowledged that the trustees were uncomfortable with the change: "But the issue had been debated and discussed sufficiently long that I think most of our board members, particularly after the passage of the legislation, began to view it more philosophically." They did not instruct the administration to lobby in opposition. Sitting members could reasonably expect reappointment if they wanted it. "So we didn't . . . we were never a force for lobbying for change. Happily our board didn't direct us to lie down in front of the train and try to stop what I think was probably inevitably going to be changed as well. So I think our board really took a high ground position on all this."

In the political environment, Tom Ryder, House deputy Republican leader, thought of the elected U of I board as peculiar and hard to explain to voters. He kidded me on the fact that the tradition of electing U of I trustees in the state at large offered political scientists a way "to determine the political bent of each district" and that its elimination would constitute a loss for my profession. But because of wide ignorance about the board candidates, "it was very difficult to cast an intelligent ballot. It was very difficult to defend the fact that we were electing those folks to that function. On the appointed, it really gives power to the governor that was not there before, but it's not a power that isn't present in all sorts of other appointments that a governor makes in this state or in others." The Democratic perspective comes from staffer Everson: "When you cut all through it, that was just an attempt to give the governor more power. The Republicans had the votes to do that. They didn't see resistance from the Urbana area legislators, and the Republicans voted for it as far as I know. So the U of I certainly never made the case that this was a bad idea."

Authorship of the proposal was not clearly determined. From the governor's staff, the "who wanted it" question was answered by Tom Livingston:

> I don't know the full story on this. I don't think anyone really does. Part of it stems out of frustrations that President Ikenberry and his crew had in the last five years. Part of it was the long-running joke that nobody knew who these people were. I think the main forces were the University and the changing nature of running for office. I think it was coming. We would look at other states and see that since the 1940s, California has appointed their regents, and I just think it was an idea that when the political climates lined up right, that it was something we were going to go with.

It seems fair to say that the governor and the president of the U of I were able to change the image of a long-practiced tradition of electing U of I trustees into an undesirable anachronism, standing in the way of getting better board members for the university's flagship public university. Had the U of I president opposed the proposal, his position doubtless would have received support from legislators around Champaign-Urbana and elsewhere. Board members would have been more conspicuous in their opposition. Democrats would have roundly resisted getting those elective positions off the ballot. But with the governor and president in harmony about the desirability, this issue was rapidly adopted on the fast track.

## Policy Venues

Baumgartner and Jones (1993) pointed out that one of the elements in their punctuated equilibrium model of policy change is the matter of policy venues. These are "the institutional locations where authoritative decisions are made concerning a given issue" (32). It is a characteristic of American politics that policy ideas can get into the system of decision-making in a variety of ways. An aspect of checks and balances is to assure varieties of access. Doubtless one of the reasons that U.S. and state senators respond to constituents is that the elected representatives who hold office in an enclave of the Senate constituency are potential rivals for the constituents' affections and the higher office. On the other hand, some problems must go through particular institutional venues. In Illinois, one of the early fights with Governor Ogilvie's budget bureau was with higher education, which believed that it could go around the governor for financial relief to the legislature. The governor vetoed the universities' requests for increases, and the legislature failed to override (Nowlan 1976, 62–77).

In 1991, when Kustra approached the governor about his restructuring ideas, he knew that any eventual change would have to go through the legislature. However, it made sense to develop the policy idea in a more controllable, if less than authoritative, venue. The logical and appropriate venue for developing and elaborating the restructure proposal was the board of higher education and its staff. Of course, the IBHE did not have the authority to make the changes that the governor wanted. Universities are governed by state statutes, so obviously changes would have to be enacted in the General Assembly. Nevertheless, the established body for providing policy expertise about higher education was the IBHE, a board equipped with a professionally qualified staff. As recounted earlier, the legislature had created the IBHE in order to serve as a buffer between itself and the state universities and to bring rationality to planning, programs, and priorities. However, the IBHE had, in May 1990, adopted its own Report of the Committee on Scope, Structure, and Productivity of Illinois Higher Education. The incumbent chair, William Browder, requested retirement, so the governor had the opportunity to appoint, as chair of the IBHE, Art Quern, an active member of the governor's transition team. But the board membership generally was not interested in structural change. According to Richard Wagner: "I think that the sense of the board members flowed from the report. Two or three of them had been on the study committee. They had dealt with the topic over a number of years. I think they generally felt that the system was working well." Pressure for change would later come from the governor's office. Quern himself was, as Kustra noted, "absolutely devoted to PQP and has been consistently throughout his chairpersonship. When this issue [restructure] surfaced, I think it is safe to say that Art joined as a reluctant supporter at most."

The result was that Edgar and Kustra needed a sympathetic venue in which to generate a proposal with a modicum of support. The solution was the creation of the Governor's Task Force on Higher Education. Besides cochairs Kustra and Quern, there were attorneys from two prominent Chicago firms, four corporate executives, and one head of a consulting firm who was executive director of reorganization efforts in Michigan and Nebraska. One member was a former U of I trustee who had been elected as a Republican. The task force reviewed a list of written references and reports, received thirty-six written responses to a solicitation by the task force, and heard oral testimony at a single public hearing from nine people, four of whom had previously provided written input. There was no intent to have public discussions and debate. The contacts were in many cases one-on-one with either Kustra or persons on his or the governor's staff. As noted in chapter 5, the task force reports were brief, and the secondhand comments about them from Sam Gove indicated a superficial process. Rod Groves labeled the group "a cheering section for Bob Kustra." It is interesting to note that although Art Quern was cochair of the task force, no other member of the IBHE nor its staff was listed as a respondent to the task force. Richard Wagner's views were not a part of the record. Moreover, the reports of the task force were addressed to the governor. So as a matter of policy action, the recommendations did "not come back to the Board of Higher Education. The Board hasn't addressed it in the immediate past," Wagner reported in 1995. He went on to say: "I wasn't involved in making the proposals. They came from a different source."

The task force provided an insulated venue. It could collect information as it wished but did not have to build a public record of that information. It did not publicly reconcile conflicting points of view. Give and take with those who offered opinions was informal. This venue selection fits with the description by Baumgartner and Jones (1993): "There are many possible institutional agendas, and for the policy makers who seek that institutional niche where decisions would likely go in their favor, none is inherently better than any other. Policy makers use manipulation of the understanding of policies as purposive tools in their search for the policy venue that will be most favorable to their interests" (36). Of course, the task force was of only limited authority. It could not adopt policy. But its report to the governor gave an appearance of coherence and support for its proposed changes from persons of substance outside the Illinois higher education community.

## Conclusion

Aspects of the restructuring of university governance, including the change from an elective to appointive board, fits Baumgartner and Jones's notion of a punctuated equilibrium model. Under the status quo, before change, there were long-existent conflicts about budget and turf, which were restrained in a system of checks and balances. Budgetary conflict was normal, incremental increases were expected, and a rather equitable distribution of benefits across the system of systems was the typical pattern.

This case study demonstrates that consensus in a policy community, here the higher education community, can be dislodged and overcome in the political stream by a determined and well-placed entrepreneur with a rival message. Moreover, it illustrates that there is no necessity for the entrepreneur to make the case for the new message in the electoral arena. In that arena, Edgar and Kustra won a mandate on issues unrelated to the substance of this case. Restructuring higher education went virtually unmentioned during the campaign. But after a sweeping win at the polls, the winners could write out their own specification of the mandate's meaning. The policy image that long had justified a higher education system of systems went practically undefended by the education community and fell away before the Edgar-Kustra challenge.

The new dimensions of conflict were to be about accountability and the restraint of or punishment for administrative bloat. Decentralization fit the national mood. Reengineering and responding to customers all fit the contemporary business buzzwords. While no measure of their impact can be estimated, it is noteworthy that "softening up" articles in major media that were critical of the universities got wide circulation just as the Edgar-Kustra task force proposals for change were first aired. Even opponents of change recognized that to defend educational bureaucrats and their salaries in that context was not politically feasible.

Ironically, the Edgar-Kustra policy imagery of overweening bureaucracy worked so well that it defeated the third item on the decision agenda, namely, to strengthen the IBHE. But to strengthen it was perceived by legislators as inconsistent with decentralization and downsizing. The IBHE became the administration's unintended target for opposition. Friendless, the proposals to strengthen the IBHE not only died, but the enthusiastic legislative supporters of community colleges almost succeeded in getting them out from under IBHE oversight because the IBHE's political leverage was so attenuated. Both chambers of the legislature voted to unshackle the community colleges. Only a governor's veto prevented that change from taking effect.

The administration was more effective reshaping the image of and policy over the U of I's elective board. Despite the elective board's more than a century of tradition and a recently vitalized Democratic Party interest in it, its elective character was changed. With support from President Ikenberry, the board was mildly but effectively labeled as partisan, a burden to voters, and comprised of people of modest significance—better a hand-picked board of heavyweights, corporate visionaries to whom standing for election would be too demeaning. Responsibility to the governor would be better than to partisan insiders and the vagaries of statewide elections.

A useful tactic for Edgar and Kustra was to find a better venue for developing and legitimating the policy proposals than the IBHE. Its members could not be dismissed, and most of them agreed with an earlier study that said the structure of higher education was just fine. Rather than fight the board, Edgar and Kustra engaged their own appointee to the board chairpersonship to additionally be a cochair of the task force. The task force thus had apparent board input and legitimacy. But actual board and staff engagement was avoided. The task force gave access to many voices but did not have to reconcile them because it made no record of their views. It could interpret those it heard from in its own way and deliver the reports and options only it preferred on the agenda. Of course, the task force could not authoritatively make policy. But it had its substance well outlined. Obviously, political failure occurred in 1993, but the political window opened in 1995. When it did, Edgar and his policy entrepreneur Kustra were ready for action with a singular proposal.

Before drawing this discussion to a close, let me go beyond the case. It pains me to note that popular support for public universities and what they do may be both thin and fragile. Who would fight back if research and public service purposes of the universities were challenged for their cost and accountability?

Professors and university administrators have not done a very convincing job of explaining to the ordinary taxpayers what, for example, professors do when they are not teaching classes. What really is the authentic workload of academic practitioners? What do they contribute to the larger society? Would the current crop of educational administrators be able to deflect and overcome destabilizing attacks from entrepreneurs with business oriented, bottom-line methods of describing university activities? What Baumgartner and Jones have pointed out as a regularity needs to be taken seriously. When policymakers shift attention to new attributes or dimensions of an existing situation, even venerable policies are subject to "policy punctuation."

# 7 | Rounding Off the Analysis

Restructuring the governance of public universities in Illinois illustrates a good deal about Illinois politics. In my way of thinking, *politics* refers to the processes for developing and resolving public issues with the authority of government. But in a mature political system, the actual order in policy-making does not always start with "developing" and end with "resolving." Kingdon (1984) rightly points out in his policy study that "events do not proceed neatly in stages, steps or phases" (215). Nevertheless, it is worthwhile to specify terms and phases to illuminate and compare policy studies. In so doing, it is my intention to get beyond simply a case study in Illinois politics.

## Theoretical Perspectives from National Studies

The essential nature of empirical studies of politics is that they proceed comparatively. The search for generalizations needs to be built upon repeated observations of similar phenomena under varying circumstances. One cannot learn all about lightening, for example, by observing a single flash. More cases and more situations reveal some characteristics as repetitive and regular, while others are particularistic or variable. Certainly the study of state politics has become much more systematic as states and their aspects have been studied comparatively.

Interestingly, however, a great deal of both theoretical and empirical knowledge about politics in this country has been developed by looking at aspects of one government, the American national government. How, for example, has one government dealt with several policies over a long time? How have several presidents and administrations pursued policy change?

The case I have studied in Illinois does not readily lend itself to direct comparison with higher education governance changes in other states. But it can be put into various frameworks of analysis that have been applied to policy-making in the United States. The rationale for doing so is not only because appropriately insightful theoretical ideas are available but also because the rich and complex character of Illinois politics does in so many respects resemble the larger setting of American domestic politics. Illinois' 11.5 million citizens occupy a heartland prairie whose boundaries are easily crossed. Its north-south distance in extraordinary. The northern boundary is north of Boston, while the southern tip between the Ohio and Mississippi Rivers is well south of Richmond, Virginia, the Confederacy's capital. As Daniel J. Elazar has explained, Illinois received infusions of all three American political subcultures—traditionalistic, moralistic, and, mostly, individualistic—since its earliest days. Its Republican and Democratic Parties are fiercely competitive, and its electoral history in American presidential conflicts during this century is remarkably closely correlated with national results (Gove and Nowlan 1996, xiv).

The structure of Illinois government features all the genius of Madisonian checks and balances (see Van Der Slik 1986a, 1986b, 1999). One can note in its several separately elected executives the evidence of Jacksonian heritage. Its civil service, code departments, board of education, and legislative service agencies are structural marks of the progressive movement. Post–World War II human rights emphases are given form in its departments on aging, professional regulation, and human rights. The constitution is modern, managerial, and permissive, and its operations in the bureaucracies are staffed with qualified careerists. Its elected politicians are mostly people for whom politics is both a business and a way of life.

The sophisticated complexity of Illinois politics, then, provides the rationale for analyzing the politics of policy-making with theoretical formulations teased out of contemporary American policy studies. The ideas I have mainly drawn upon have come particularly from John Kingdon (1984), Charles O. Jones (1977, 1995), and Frank R. Baumgartner and Bryan D. Jones (1991, 1993; see also Jones, Baumgartner, and True 1998).

## Policy Study in Review

It was not the higher education policy community that put the restructuring of higher education on the agenda. To the contrary, it was imposed upon the policy community over its members' objections. Agitation for governance change was kept alive on a couple of state university campuses until a change in the political stream brought Jim Edgar and Bob Kustra into the executive branch, and together they placed a corporate visionary, Art Quern, into the position of chair of the IBHE. Problem recognition—the notion that public university governance needed to be restructured—emerged from the minds and inclinations of those political players based upon their early adult experiences and ideas. As was noted by Kingdon as commonplace, agenda setting in this instance followed a conventional top-down model.

Focusing events are not numerous or obvious. There was no crisis in any of the systems or even at any of the campuses. Nothing resembling the days of rage on the campuses during 1970 put this issue at the forefront. Respondents disagree about whether or not the firing of a campus president at Jim Edgar's alma mater was or was not a triggering event. It may have been a reminder to the governor of his earlier frustrations with one element of the system of systems. It was less than a cause célèbre.

Clearly, there was an available policy entrepreneur in Lieutenant Governor Bob Kustra. He had undeniable academic credentials, wide university experience in the state, and the resources of visibility, time, energy, and staff support to pursue the issue. Doubtless, he perceived a problem that he believed needed a solution. He could use the problem to enlarge his political visibility in communities of the state potentially sympathetic to change, improving his prospects for future political electability for statewide office. From the analyst's perspective, it seems apt to say that Kustra and Edgar were enamored of a particular policy solution. To put it into place, they needed to identify and articulate the problem to be solved.

The political leaders had a policy solution to a problem that most of the policy community did not acknowledge. Therefore, instead of specifying an endless supply of alternative solutions and fighting for them, those in the policy community checked out the political viability of the governor's proposal and judged it likely to lose. In 1993, it did, and it remained off the agenda during 1994.

Despite a legislative defeat, the governor did move to muzzle the objections of policy leaders in the two target systems, the Board of Regents and the Board of Governors. Others in the education community did not defend the targets. By the time that the issue was back on the decision agenda, changes in the board memberships of those systems denied the system heads support for their arguments against the governor's proposals. The near silence of those with stakes in the status quo was palpable.

That the 1994 election opened the window for the governor's governance proposals was widely recognized. At that point, a key policy player, President Ikenberry of the U of I, could see the advantage of supporting the administration if it would reshape one rather small element in the policy proposal—eliminate the union baggage associated with making Sangamon State a campus of the U of I. The governor and his legislature allies could and did complete that change with fast-track tactics.

In the legislature, the fast-track tactics of Republicans consolidated the support of their legislative leaders and rank and file members with the governor. Fast track inhibited the articulation of legislative alternatives and gave a substantial number of new Republican legislators party cover for voting in support of the governor and the legislative leaders on a policy about which they had little understanding. The result was not so much a substantively partisan vote as it was a tactically partisan one.

There were few "other interests" with stakes in the issue. It was not a tax and spend or jobs issue to draw attention from peak interest groups. It did not stimulate grass roots opposition for legislators. The private universities and colleges were silent. The faculty union at Sangamon State was, as union lobbyist Ettinger said, "roadkill on the fast track." The single active local community was Springfield, whose boosters mostly needed to convince the U of I administration that taking SSU in was positive for the university in the long run.

Charles O. Jones was on to something when he pointed out the significance of an inherited agenda. Edgar won office with no mandate, partisan minorities in both legislative chambers, and a restrictive set of fiscal constraints. However, after Republicans gained a majority in the Senate in 1993, and a solid reelection victory accompanied by a complementary majority in the House in 1995, the Edgar administration could and did achieve a high degree of agenda congruity with Republican legislative leaders. This is outside the range of Jones's findings. None of the presidents he examined obtained a second-term reelection that brought with it high agenda congruity. Edgar did achieve that and used it successfully after his reelection. It is a phenomenon that bears watching for with presidents and other governors.

The restructure of higher education seems to fit with Jones's notions about ambitious decision-making and speculative augmentation. The administration went for major change, but it had only ambiguous estimates about what would be accomplished thereby. Perhaps that should not be surprising. Higher education scholars lack clear findings on which to anticipate unambiguous outcomes from institutional shifts in governance (see Hearn and Griswold 1994; Marcus 1997). Different players expected different future outcomes. There was no specification of performance objectives to confirm success or failure. No rationally determined enumeration of consequences was estimated in advance. To the contrary, the political window was open, and the political proponents knew instinctively how they wanted to use the opportunity, in hopes that desirable consequences would follow. Responses from those on the governor's side indicate that they were looking for a variety of results—localizing interests and board memberships, competition for students and on tuition rates, greater accountability, and reduction in the educationist bureaucracies.

The restructuring of higher education in Illinois has many of the marks of the policy punctuation theory outlined by Baumgartner and Jones. It was a new policy package, breaking the enduring system of systems, replacing a century-old tradition of elective board members for the state's flagship public university, and attempting an unprecedented centralization of power in the IBHE. The first two measures passed on the fast track, but the last was entangled in the new dimensions of conflict that the advocates for change set in motion, and it projected the "wrong image" in violation of the new orthodoxy favoring localization of control.

The old dimensions of conflict had to do with scarcity and checks and balances within the system of systems. The new emphasized accountability of each campus to its own board, the capacity for the school to meet and respond to local-regional opportunities, and the local determination of what school priorities will be. Decision-making by the customers and clients of the universities would drive their policies, not external checks and balances.

Interestingly, by raising the specter of bureaucratic bloat successfully enough to disarm the BOR and BOG, the climate was created that defeated the administration's interest in strengthening the capacity of the IBHE to rein in not only the smaller schools but also certainly the evermore dominant position and re-sources of the U of I. The IBHE went away from the 1995 legislative session with its powers legally undiminished, but its credibility in tatters. It was unable on its own to prevent passage of a bill to set the community college system free from IBHE oversight. It took a governor's veto to do that.

The Edgar administration, with active facilitation by President Ikenberry, succeeded in changing the image of a democratically elected board for the U of I into an anachronism marred by partisan small-mindedness. No longer a good example of Jacksonian democracy, it was seen as a bar to high-minded, vision-ary trustees of national or international reputation who could give direction to the state's flagship university. The change would bring its governance into con-formity to the predominant fashion of American university governance.

Baumgartner and Jones suggested the relevance of venue shopping. The ob-vious venue for developing the administration's proposals for university gover-nance was at IBHE, with the sophisticated assistance of its professional staff. But that was a venue committed to the status quo and habituated to dealing with the old dimensions of policy conflict: fiscal security and checks and balances. A newly created venue, the governor's task force, was unencumbered by tradition, and its hand-picked membership was experienced with corporate change and restruc-turing. The task force was willing to "hear" from anyone with a point of view but had no responsibility to build and balance a public record, as might the IBHE. The task force proposed a framework, an outline, not a well-rationalized study or argument for changes. Its initial report was accompanied by two substantive softening-up journalistic treatments that questioned the accountability of the state's universities and their commitment to undergraduate education. The venue change helped mute the IBHE's voice in behalf of the status quo and gave the governor and his administration control over the shape and extent of the changes to be advocated.

It is, of course, possible that Edgar and Kustra might have achieved their objective eventually by simply persevering, working at the appointment of new BOR and BOG board members committed to their position. But the political shift in the Republican landslide election of 1994 opened the window of politi-cal opportunity to rewrite policy legislatively. Republican control in the legisla-ture enabled Edgar and Kustra to give the U of I a third campus, unencumbered by its unionized faculty bargaining unit.

While only a few Republican legislators felt strong stakes in the restructure, they were sufficiently committed to the new policy images about higher educa-tion restructuring to reject any changes in the IBHE that smacked of "super board" powers. That would not play and could not be ratified even by the governor's reformist allies. No one would so much as introduce a bill to that effect. To the contrary, it was the governor who had to call a halt to decentralization by using his veto when legislators were willing to go beyond his proposals and cut com-munity colleges free from IBHE oversight.

## Thanks for Theory

The opening chapter offered simply a chronological account of the restructure, with emphasis on 1993 and 1995 journalistic reports of who did what, when and how. Viewed in that light, the case study is unique and filled with particularistic details. Certainly, there are specifics to any case study that may be unmatched elsewhere.

What I hope I have shown is that this case is illustrative of generalizations about policy-making in the United States and that looking deeply even into singular cases is a way to elaborate and confirm larger theoretical generalizations. There is a great deal of political complexity that is accessible in this state as well as others that can contribute to wider understanding about "the processes for the developing and resolving of public issues with the authority of government," my definition of politics. Students and, perhaps, too many citizens easily dismiss our politicians as greedy simpletons, blinded by ego and insensitive to citizen desires. None of those things are evidenced in this case study.

To the contrary, it was noteworthy that the political flexibility of the players in this matter was broad because the matter did not stimulate the interests of either many citizens or special interest groups. What I did find was political players with varying degrees of political leverage who perceived the implications of the status quo and that changes from it would have authentic policy consequences. Some believed the changes would produce better results than no change. Others disagreed. The change agents in this situation, primarily the governor and lieutenant governor, worked diligently and skillfully at their solution to a problem that most higher education leaders would not acknowledge or held to be of minimal significance.

It is true that there was not much direct citizen involvement in this major policy change. It should be acknowledged that most issues do not move most citizens to direct action most of the time. That is why our system of representative democracy depends upon elected leaders, usually executives and legislators, to make major policy calls. But we expect them to care about citizen views and to be responsive to popular interests as they act in our behalf. In this case, one interest group, the faculty union at Sangamon State, was a clear loser in the policy determination. It found itself with few allies and limited resources, and it was unprepared regarding policy alternatives and overcome by partisan fast-track tactics. But it did have advocates, and it did have access to the decision process. Additional citizen input was exemplified by community efforts in Springfield to get SSU into the U of I system. That effort was rewarded with success. Undeniably, policy shifts create winners and losers.

In addition to individual winners—Edgar and Kustra as the obvious examples—several institutions gained substantially. In my judgment, the big winner was Northern Illinois University. Already large and diverse, with numerous doctoral programs and a law school, a suburban educational center, and the beginnings of a big-time athletic program, it is now free to pursue the opportunities of the educational marketplace. Previously, President La Tourette felt inhibited when he compared his presidency to that of Stanley Ikenberry at the U of I. Northern is the most accessible public university for Illinois students who live forty miles or so away from DeKalb, in the greater Chicago metropolitan area. NIU can confer not only undergraduate degrees. It has a wide and growing array of graduate programs. Northern is well situated to serve the lifelong learning interests of a growing population in the richest and most education-oriented region of Illinois.

The University of Illinois was a major winner. It is arguable that the Sangamon State addition is only a mixed blessing, costly and an administrative burden in the near term. Over the long term, however, it has significant potential, with a campus of over six hundred acres, within the capital city. Importantly, as part of the U of I rather than Southern Illinois University, the flagship university enhances its access and service to the state of Illinois, and there will be long and continuing political returns generated thereby. The U of I got its appointed board, and that board will be a magnet for membership by persons of high status, financial resources, and cutting-edge knowledge useful to keeping the U of I on the forefront of public education in the United States and the world.

Less conspicuous, but real winners, are the community colleges. They found to their surprise that they can exercise influence on state legislators and that state legislators have more community colleges in their constituencies than state universities. That lesson was likewise learned at the IBHE, whose leadership will need to give community college educational and capital development priorities greater respect than perhaps they have in the past.

The obvious losers were the board members, chancellors, and staffs of the regency and governors systems. They were dissolved, dispersed, and, in a couple of cases, exiled. Less obviously, but certainly a loser, was the SIU system. It missed a chance because of weak leadership to add a Springfield campus to its system and to deny that benefit to the U of I. The population stagnation in southern Illinois continues, eroding its legislative base, and the dynamism of SIU in the 1960s and 1970s is no longer conspicuous in the state. The place of SIU-Carbondale as "second jewel" in the early master plans is likely to give way effectively to Northern Illinois University. SIU's future significance may increasingly depend upon the development of its Edwardsville campus.

Clearly, the IBHE took its lumps. It was out of the loop when Edgar and Kustra made their foray against the system of systems. It was cast as a power grabber in the legislature and on the other campuses, but it was totally unsuccessful in gaining statutory authority to better coordinate the now increasingly independent universities. It was a lonely opponent to the attempt to take the community college system out from under its oversight. Instead of an earlier role as balancer in a web of checks and balances, IBHE is on the wrong side of an image of accountability to diverse boards and decentralized educational control.

The other six universities—Eastern, Western, Illinois State, Northeastern, Governors, and Chicago State—may or may not be winners. They will have to both compete and cooperate to get students and resources. Their skill in dealing with secondary schools and community colleges and their graduates may be highly important to further success. Whether or not they can compete at distance learning with the bigger state schools remains to be seen. One form that inter-university competition will take is in lobbying the legislature. Whether or not the IBHE can perform as an effective buffer in that competitive legislative arena is difficult to predict, but it certainly bears watching.

Public officials elected to high office do make a difference in the way we are organized and governed. They do act on attitudes and policy positions formed earlier in their careers. Nameless, faceless bureaucrats certainly have substantive roles to play in policy operations, but elected officials do call the tune and do exercise great discretion over the policy agenda. Elections change the power structure and the players, bringing about significant policy consequences. In fact, when one political party gains control of the separated institutions of our Madisonian system, it can overcome checks and balances to bring about significant policy punctuations. Indeed, when such elections occur after a period of divided party governance, we should expect policy punctuations to accompany them. Perhaps this is nothing new, but in an era of low public trust in the responsiveness of our politicians, perhaps it deserves attention and respect.

# Bibliography
# Index

# Bibliography

Allee, Kelly. 1994. "Weaver Hopes New Legislature Will Revive Bill to Abolish BGU." *Charleston Times Courier,* 24 December.

———. 1995. "Weaver: BGU, Rives Dispute Prompted Elimination Bill." *Charleston Times Courier,* March.

Atkins, Thomas. 1993. "SIU Officials Appear Eager to Merge with Sangamon State." *Illinois Times,* 24–30 June.

Baumgartner, Frank R., and Bryan D. Jones. 1991. "Agenda Dynamics and Policy Subsystems." *Journal of Politics* 53.4 (November): 1044–74.

———. 1993. *Agendas and Instability in American Politics.* Chicago: University of Chicago Press.

Bowen, Frank M., Kathy Reeves Bracco, Patrick M. Callan, Joni E. Finney, Richard C. Richardson Jr., and William Trombley. 1997. *State Structures for the Governance of Higher Education: A Comparative Study.* San Jose: California Higher Education Policy Center.

Braybrooke, David, and Charles E. Lindblom. 1963. *A Strategy of Decision.* New York: Free Press.

Burnham, Walter Dean. 1991. "Critical Realignment: Dead or Alive?" In *The End of Realignment? Interpreting American Eras,* edited by Byron E. Schafer. Madison: University of Wisconsin Press, 101–39.

Cobb, Roger W., and Charles D. Elder. 1983. *Participation in American Politics: The Dynamics of Agenda-Building.* Baltimore: Johns Hopkins University Press.

Coleman, Glen. 1992. "Higher Ed on Collision Course." *Crain's Chicago Business,* 8 June, 1, 21–32.

Daniels, Lee. 1995a. "Illinois Agenda Was Amazing Achievement." *State Journal-Register,* 12 March, Letters from Readers section.

———. 1995b. "Legislative Update" Newsletter. Legislative Printing Unit, June.

Eldredge, Niles, and Stephen J. Gould. 1972. "Punctuated Equilibria: An Alternative to Phyletic Gradualism." In *Models in Paleobiology,* edited by T. M. J. Schopf. San Francisco: Freeman, Cooper, 82–115.

Everson, David H., and Samuel K. Gove. 1993. "Interest Groups in Illinois: The Political Microcosm of the Nation." In *Interest Groups in the Midwestern States,* edited by Ronald J. Hrebenar and Clive S. Thomas. Ames: Iowa State University Press, 20–49.

Falcone, Pete. 1995. "Kustra Predicts Majority Likely to Eliminate ISU Governing Board. *The Pantagraph,* 13 January.

Finke, Doug. 1993. "House Committee Rejects SSU's Merger with U of I." *State Journal-Register,* 6 May.

Finke, Doug, and Jay Fitzgerald. 1993. "Edgar's Higher Ed Plan Sparks Fight." *State Journal-Register,* 19 February.

Finke, Doug, and Doug Pokorski. 1995. "Senate Votes to Make SSU Part of U of I." *State Journal-Register,* 10 February.

Fitzgerald, Jay. 1993a. "Higher Education Proposal Faces Uphill Climb." *State Journal-Register,* 22 April.

———. 1993b. "SSU/U of I Merger on Back Burner." *State Journal-Register,* 4 April.

———. 1993c. "U of I President Still Cool to Merger." *State Journal-Register,* 12 May.

Floyd, Carol Everly. 1992. "Centralization and Decentralization of State Decision Making for Public Universities: Illinois 1960–1990." In *History of Higher Education Annual 1992,* edited by Harold S. Wechsler. University Park: Pennsylvania State University, 101–18.

Furman, James M. 1987. "Higher Education's System of Systems: It Works." *Illinois Issues,* November, 18–21.

Gove, Samuel K., and Carol Everly Floyd. 1973. "The Politics of Public Higher Education in Illinois." *AAUP Bulletin* 59 (September): 287–93.

Gove, Samuel K., and James D. Nowlan. 1996. *Illinois Politics and Government: The Expanding Metropolitan Frontier.* Lincoln: University of Nebraska Press.

Governor's Task Force on Higher Education. 1992. First Report on Governance. Springfield: Office of the Lieutenant Governor, 15 June.

———. 1993. Final Report. Springfield: Office of the Governor, January.

Greer, Darryl G. 1986. "Politics and Higher Education: The Strategy of State-Level Coordination and Policy Implementation." In *Policy Controversies in Higher Education,* edited by Samuel K. Gove and Thomas M. Stauffer. New York: Greenwood Press, 27–49.

Grossman, Ron, Carol Jouzaitis, and Charles Leroux. 1992. "Degrees of Neglect." *Chicago Tribune,* 21–25 June.

Halperin, Jennifer. 1993. "Statewide Property Tax Caps Top Gov. Edgar's Agenda." *Illinois Issues,* March, 10–12.

Harris, Douglas B. 1998. "The Rise of the Public Speakership." *Political Science Quarterly* 113.2 (summer): 193–212.

Hartmark, Leif S., and Edward R. Hines. 1986. "Politics and Policy in Higher Education: Reflections on the Status of the Field." In *Policy Controversies in Higher Education,* edited by Samuel K. Gove and Thomas M. Stauffer. New York: Greenwood Press, 3–26.

Hawthorne, Michael. 1994. "Higher Ed Governance Could Be in for Changes," and "UI-Sangamon Merger Plan to Get New State Push." *Champaign-Urbana News-Gazette,* 20 December.

Hearn, James C., and Carolyn P. Griswold. 1994. "State-Level Centralization and Policy Innovation in U.S. Postsecondary Education." *Educational Evaluation and Policy Analysis* 16.2 (summer): 161–90.

"Higher Education: Other Views on Its Governance System (and Other Issues)." 1988. *Illinois Issues,* January, 21–26.

"Higher Education's System of Systems: Reform Rebuttal." 1988. *Illinois Issues,* February, 14.

House Higher Education Committee Hearing. 1993. Springfield: Illinois House of Representatives, 11 March.

Ikenberry, Stanley O. 1995. Letter to Richard D. Wagner. 8 February.

Illinois Board of Higher Education. 1967. Report of the Special Committee on New Senior Institutions. Springfield: IBHE, December.

———. 1990. Report of the Committee on Scope, Structure, and Productivity in Illinois Higher Education. *An Action Agenda for Illinois Higher Education: Improving Quality, Cost Effectiveness, and Accountability in the 1990s.* Springfield: IBHE, 1 May.

———. 1997. *Data Book on Illinois Higher Education.* Springfield: IBHE.

Jones, Bryan D., Frank R. Baumgartner, and James L. True. 1998. "Policy Punctuations: U.S. Budget Authority, 1947–1995." *The Journal of Politics* 60.1 (February): 1–33.

Jones, Charles O. 1977. *An Introduction to the Study of Public Policy.* 2d ed. North Scituate, Mass.: Duxbury Press.

———. 1995. *Separate but Equal Branches: Congress and the Presidency.* Chatham, N.J.: Chatham House.

Kelly, Sean Q. 1994. "Punctuated Change and the Era of Divided Government." In *New Perspectives on American Politics,* edited by Lawrence C. Dodd and Calvin Jillson. Washington, D.C.: CQ Press, 162–90.

Kingdon, John W. 1984. *Agendas, Alternatives, and Public Policies.* Boston: Little, Brown.

Lasswell, Harold D. 1936. *Politics: Who Gets What, When, How.* Glencoe, Ill.: Free Press.

Lewis, Dan A., and Shadd Maruna. 1996. "The Politics of Education." In *Politics in the American States: A Comparative Analysis,* edited by Virginia Gray and Herbert Jacob. 6th ed. Washington, D.C.: CQ Press, 438–77.

Mahtesian, Charles. 1995. "Higher Ed: The No-Longer-Sacred Cow." *Governing,* July, 20–26.

Marcus, Lawrence R. 1997. "Restructuring State Higher Education Governance Patterns." *Review of Higher Education* 20.4 (summer): 399–418.

Matsler, Franklin G., and Edward R. Hines. 1987. *State Policy Formation in Illinois Higher Education.* Normal, Ill.: Center for Higher Education, Illinois State University.

Mattmiller, Brian. 1993. "SIU Won't Inherit a Campus." *Southern Illinoisan,* 28 January.

Monroe, Alan D. 1982. "Elections: Political Culture, Public Opinion, Sectionalism, and Voting." In *Illinois: Political Processes and Governmental Performance,* edited by Edgar C. Crane. Dubuque: Kendall/Hunt, 156–66.

National Commission on Excellence in Education. 1983. *A Nation at Risk.* Washington, D.C.: The Commission.

Nowlan, James D. 1976. *The Politics of Higher Education: Lawmakers and the Academy in Illinois.* Urbana: University of Illinois Press.

Nowlan, James D., and Samuel K. Gove. 1991. "The Politics of Education in Illinois." In *Inside State Government in Illinois,* edited by James D. Nowlan. Chicago: Neltnor House, 103–36.

Nowlan, James D., Christopher O. Ross, and Mildred A. Schwartz. 1984. *The University of Illinois Trustees: "Invisible" Statewide Candidates.* Urbana: Institute of Government and Public Affairs, University of Illinois.

Pensoneau, Taylor. 1997. *Governor Richard Ogilvie: In the Interest of the State.* Carbondale: Southern Illinois University Press.

Pokorski, Doug. 1993a. "BOR Head: Don't Change Higher Ed Structure." *State Journal-Register,* 26 March.

———. 1993b. "Can SSU Maintain Its Identity under U of I?" *State Journal-Register,* 1 April.

———. 1993c. "Democrats Attack Edgar's Higher Ed Plan." *State Journal-Register,* 12 March.

———. 1993d. "Higher Ed Plan Splits Educators, Legislators." *State Journal-Register,* 28 January.

———. 1995a. "Edgar Signs Higher Education Measure." *State Journal-Register,* 1 March.

———. 1995b. "Panel Oks Joining SSU with U of I." *State Journal-Register,* 2 February.

———. 1995c. "Senate Committee Approves Plan to Reorganize University System." *State Journal-Register,* 8 February.

———. 1995d. "SSU Joining U of I Soon, Kustra Says." *State Journal-Register,* 4 January.

Pollock, James. 1993. "New Faces in the Senate." *Illinois Issues,* January, 25–27.

Redfield, Kent. 1995. *Cash Clout: Political Money in Illinois Legislative Elections.* Springfield: Institute for Public Affairs, University of Illinois at Springfield.

Riker, William H. 1982. *Liberalism Against Populism.* Prospect Heights, Ill.: Waveland Press.

Ripley, Randall B., and Grace A. Franklin. 1991. *Congress, the Bureaucracy, and Public Policy.* 5th ed. Pacific Grove, Calif.: Brooks/Cole.

Rubin, Alissa J. 1997. "'Fast Track' and China Policy: Could This Be the Year?" *Congressional Quarterly Weekly Report,* 18 January, 162–66.

Ryan, George H. 1997. *Illinois Handbook of Government 1997–1998.* Springfield: State of Illinois.

Schafer, Tom. 1998. *Meeting the Challenge: The Edgar Administration, 1991–1999.* Springfield, Ill.: State of Illinois.

Schattschneider, E. E. 1960. *The Semi-Sovereign People.* New York: Holt, Rinehart, and Winston.

Scobell, Beverly. 1993. "Taming the Higher Education Beast." *Illinois Issues,* August-September, 43–44.

Sinclair, Barbara. 1997. *Unorthodox Lawmaking: New Legislative Processes in the U.S. Congress.* Washington, D.C.: CQ Press.

Somit, Albert. 1987. "Illinois' System of Systems: Time for a Change in Higher Education." *Illinois Issues,* October, 20–24.

*State Journal-Register.* 1990. Editorial, 11 May.

Thompson, Don. 1992. "Task Force Weighs Regency System Merits." *The Pantagraph,* 14 June.

———. 1994. "Governing Board Demise on Edgar's Back Burner." *The Pantagraph,* 12 October.

Thurber, James A. 1995. "Remaking Congress after the Electoral Earthquake of 1994." In *Remaking Congress: Change and Stability in the 1990s,* edited by James A. Thurber and Roger H. Davidson. Washington, D.C.: CQ Press , 1–27.

Van Der Slik, Jack. 1986a. "Bargain Politics: Second Best Results." *Illinois Issues,* August-September, 74–75.

———. 1986b. "Madison Would Have Loved Illinois Government." *Chicago Tribune,* 12 September.

———. 1995. *One for All and All for Illinois: Representing the Land of Lincoln in Congress.* Foreword by Paul Simon. Springfield, Ill.: Sangamon State University.

———. 1999. "Representational Democracy Is Messy, but Our Government Works." *Illinois Issues,* January, 6–7.

Wagner, Richard D. 1995. "Higher Education Restructure Proposal." Paper presented to the Senate Higher Education Committee, 7 February, Springfield, Illinois.

Wheeler, Charles N., III. 1991a. "Critical, Crowded Agenda." *Illinois Issues,* January, 8–9.

———. 1991b. "'Hurricane' Edgar: Rookie Governor's First Session." *Illinois Issues,* August-September, 10–12.

———. 1992. Electoral Politics Supersede Fiscal Policy." *Illinois Issues,* August-September, 8–11.

———. 1993a. "Edgar's Midterm Menu." *Illinois Issues,* February, 6–7.

———. 1993b. "Making Deals Illinois-Style." *Illinois Issues,* August-September, 8–10.

———. 1995. "Gov. Edgar's Address Rehashes Standard Republican Agenda." *Illinois Issues,* February, 8–9.

Williams, Amy E. 1995. "Local Lawmakers Hail Edgar's Speech." *State Journal-Register,* 13 January.

Wilson, James Q. 1973. *Political Organizations.* New York: Basic Books.

Wurth, Julie. 1992. "Firsts Aside, UI Board Makeup Changed Little." *Champaign-Urbana News-Gazette,* 5 November.

———. 1993. "Sangamon State as UI Campus? Edgar Likes It." *Champaign-Urbana News-Gazette,* 29 January.

Zumeta, William. 1998. "Public University Accountability to the State in the Late Twentieth Century: Time for a Rethinking?" *Policy Studies Review* 15.4 (winter): 5–22.

# Index

**Jack R. Van Der Slik** was the director of the Illinois Legislative Studies Center from 1983 to 1998. He is the author of *American Legislative Processes* and coauthor, with Kent Redfield, of *Lawmaking in Illinois.* His most recent book is *One for All and All for Illinois,* a study of the Illinois congressional delegation. He is the founding editor of the *Almanac of Illinois Politics,* which he edited biennially from 1990 to 1998. His academic degrees are from Calvin College, Western Michigan University, and Michigan State University.